# FORWARD OBSERVER

# OBSERVER

BY

EDWIN V. WESTRATE

*Published by* **THE BLAKISTON COMPANY,** *Philadelphia*

*Distributed by* **E. P. DUTTON & CO., INC.,** *New York*

# NOTE

Every combat incident recorded here is authentic but, for military reasons, the real identity of the participants, their outfits and the exact location of their exploits may not be revealed as yet. So the names Kennard, Hallon, Johns, Warren, Byrnes and the rest seemed as good as any. Names of field commanders and of Fort Sill officers mentioned are, of course, their own.

I wish to acknowledge especially my great indebtedness to Lieutenant-Colonel Percy Thompson, who was *there*—and won the Silver Star for gallantry in action—and to Major Glenn S. Hubbard of the staff of the Field Artillery School for their invaluable assistance in the preparation of this book.

The Author.

# FORWARD OBSERVER

# I

KENNARD—JAMES KENNARD, first lieutenant, Field Artillery—was brought back to the United States from Africa on a stretcher, by airplane. His radio operator, Barney Johns, technician 5, occupied another stretcher on the same plane. They had been wounded within a few minutes of each other somewhere near Bizerte while on a special mission they had undertaken together. It was the second time Johns had been wounded, the fourth for Kennard. Jack Warren, who had been Kennard's first instrument corporal, was in the same hospital when they arrived. He had preceded them by a week or two, both as to the time he was wounded—his second time, also—and his return across the Atlantic.

One day, after Kennard was able to sit up in bed for a few minutes at a time, a general came to the hospital and pinned a Distinguished Service Cross on him. He did not seem particularly excited about it. The only time his face lighted was when he was told Johns was receiving the same decoration. Warren already was wearing the Silver Star for Bravery, awarded him in Africa some days before he was hit by the four machine-gun bullets which had sent him back to the United States.

These three and one other who is still in Africa had been the original members of one of those little-known, almost fabulous groups which haunt the farthest reaches of the battle fronts with Death riding their shoulders at every step —the forward observer details. Kennard's quartet had been the forward observer detail of Battery C, ——th Battalion of light field artillery—105 millimeter howitzers—operating in direct support of the infantry.

When they were well enough to move about in wheel chairs, Warren and Johns spent most of their time around

Kennard's bed. Their attitude toward each other was not much that of officer and subordinates. They seemed to be just intimate friends with a deep respect for each other and the comradeship of men who have been through hell together.

Kennard looks considerably older than he is. He was very young when he landed in Africa but so much happened to him and around him and because of him that he aged many years in the six months between November 8, 1942 and the May day when the Americans catapulted into Bizerte. To a lesser degree, the same is true of Warren and Johns.

When the three are together, they sometimes reminisce but mostly they talk about going back to the outfit. Kennard discounts completely the dismal medical opinion which questions whether he will emerge from the hospital without a permanent limp, much less return to combat. He himself says he will be as good as new, if for no other reason than that he has to be.

He will, too. He is that kind. It takes his kind to do the job he learned so well and he knows the American Army does not yet have enough of him to finish the enormous task still ahead.

There are only four men in a forward observer detail—the forward observer, who is a commissioned officer (usually the battery reconnaissance officer), and three enlisted men—an instrument corporal, a wire telephone operator and a radio operator. In the North African campaign, American casualties were less than 20 per cent of the total American forces engaged. During the same period, Kennard's detail suffered more than 300 per cent casualties, not to mention minor wounds which kept men off duty only a day or two.

That is what forward observer service is like.

This is not the story of the Tunisian campaign. It is just the story—as it was told from hospital cot and wheel chair—of Lieutenant Kennard and the men of his detail and what happened to them as they learned how to make war.

# II

KENNARD AND RICK HALLON became friends under rather peculiar circumstances. It began during a Yale-Army football game. Kennard was a back on the Yale eleven and Hallon, then a First Classman, was playing end for West Point.

About the middle of the third period, Hallon leaped high to snag a short forward pass. When he hit the ground, half the Yale team was on him. He was tackled instantly and went down in a curious, twisted fall with a Yale man toppling across him. If they had crashed as they were, Hallon's neck almost inevitably would have been broken. Kennard saw this as he dove into the play and he managed to grab Hallon with a lunging heave which straightened him out before he struck the ground. The West Pointer's breath was knocked out of him but he was grinning when he looked up at Kennard whose expression still was a trifle strained.

"Thanks," Hallon gasped. "Glad—to have met you—head on."

Kennard pulled him to his feet, slapped him on the back and went back to his post.

After the game, Hallon looked him up. "I just thought I'd like to know you," he said simply.

It became one of those friendships which is possible only between men who think in the same straight lines and develop a profound respect and liking for each other. Their planned careers were far apart and, in the brief years before the war they saw each other only infrequently but the tie between them grew increasingly strong.

They had one common interest which held more significance than either could imagine. After he was graduated from West Point, Hallon went to the field artillery. Kennard, too, specialized in artillery at the Yale ROTC and he had a reserve officer's commission in that branch when he collected his university sheepskin.

He was called into active service as a second lieutenant in 1941. He had hoped to serve with Hallon's outfit but the battalion officer complement was full and he was assigned elsewhere. He did not see Hallon again until he was sent to Fort Sill.

So far as practicable, all field artillery officers in the United States Army pass through the Field Artillery School at Fort Sill before they are okayed for combat duty. Ever since the School of Fire was established there in 1911, that field artillery training center has held high rank in military circles. Today, under the guidance of Brigadier General Jesmond D. Balmer, the young commandant who took the reins early in 1942, it is the greatest field artillery school in the world.

To meet the tremendous emergency, the numerous courses necessary in the many-faceted technique of field artillery were streamlined for maximum speed of wartime training, consistent with combat efficiency, and they are taught by a staff of the most brilliant and competent instructors available. These courses at the FAS are extremely tough and the men who conduct them have ice water in their veins, for which the country should be profoundly grateful. They operate on the simple premise that any officer who does not prove to them his worthiness to lead men into battle cannot receive their stamp of approval. As a result, those who do not pass the exacting FAS tests usually find themselves "promoted" to innocuous desk jobs where they have no chance to kill any of the men who happen to serve under them.

Hallon was a captain, taking the Battery Officers Course at Fort Sill when Kennard arrived for his own BOC. As the FAS courses keep the students busy from dawn to approximately midnight six days a week, they did not have much time to be together in the two weeks which still remained of Hallon's course but they took advantage of such time as they had, both still hoping for eventual service in the same outfit.

After he returned to his battery, Hallon did something about it, especially after Kennard, now a first lieutenant, wrote of his ambition to become a forward observer. About the time Kennard was informed he had satisfied the FAS demands, he received his orders to proceed from Fort Sill, upon completion of his course, directly to the camp where Hallon's division was in training and, specifically, to report to Hallon's battalion commander. A letter from Hallon came also.

"It's fixed for your assignment to the battery," it read. "My RO [1] has been upped to captain. You will replace him and you can forward observe from here to Berlin and Tokyo. Be seeing you."

Organizing and training the forward observer detail is the personal duty of the reconnaissance officer. When Kennard joined Hallon, he discovered he would have to start from scratch as the previous detail had been dissolved. The instrument corporal and wire telephone operator had been sent to Officers' Candidate School and the radio operator had become a sergeant.

"That's the kind of men you want for an FO detail," said Kennard, "fellows who are definitely officer material. They have to be well above average for the job. They must be husky to be able to stand up under the grind but they have to have more than muscle. They must be intelligent, alert, aggressive and able to think on their feet because most of the time they're entirely on their own in tight spots. Good personalities help, too. The members of an FO detail have to get along with a lot of strangers, especially the infantry.

"Our big problem was time. The division was well along in its training. It had less than two months before maneuvers and, after that, it was practically certain we would be on our

[1] Reconnaissance Officer.

way. So we had to choose the men for the detail in a hurry, but we were lucky."

Among the replacements Hallon's battery had received, they found Jack Warren who had been taking an engineering course at college when he enlisted. He was big, smart, congenial and had the qualities of leadership. He was pegged for the instrument corporal.

Also among the new men was Barney Johns, an intelligent young husky with an irrepressible sense of humor. He had gone into radio when circumstances had forced him to abandon an electrical engineering course. He was put down as the detail's radio operator. For the wire telephone operator, Hal Furman was lifted from the battery's regular telephone men. He had been a lineman for the American Telephone and Telegraph Company before Pearl Harbor. He was a stolid, serious-minded individual, a year or two older than the others. "He looked," said Kennard, "like a man who would go through hell and high water to carry out any assignment handed him—and he was."

"Lieutenant Kennard didn't give us time to draw our breath," said Warren from his wheel chair. "As soon as the detail was announced, he called us together and told us that, from then on, we would ignore all battery calls except morning assembly and retreat as we weren't going to see much of the battery. He was right. We didn't. We hardly had time for mess."

"We had too much ground to cover," said Kennard. "The members of the forward observer detail had to know more than all the other enlisted men of the battery combined. Next to being expert in his own particular line, each man had to become expert in all the other detail jobs, including that of the officer—especially the officer—and had to have all the basic knowledge that demanded.

"They had to learn the fundamentals of gunnery, how to handle a one-o-five howitzer, how to lay it and how to figure firing data. The chances were they never would have to touch a gun in action but they had to know what a one-o-five can do and how it acts.

"They had to learn sensing. That's judging, in terms of yards, just how far the adjusting bursts miss the target—short or over and right or left. It is one of an observer's most important duties. The Field Artillery School at Fort Sill insists the target should be hit on the second round. With accurate sensing, you can do it.

"Fixing the exact location of a target is just as important. It's simpler than it used to be. Now the artillery selects what is called a base point, some target or any point in enemy territory which is easily seen. All field pieces using the same base point are trained on it as soon as they are in position. Once the firing data for that is determined, it is the basis for all other computations. That makes it easy to shift from target to target because the locations of all targets are reported with reference to the base point as, for instance, by saying, 'Base point is three hundred right, four hundred over.' Judging the location of a target that way is a good deal like sensing. It takes good eyes, common sense and a lot of practice. We were at it every day out on the range.

"One of the most important and most difficult of all things the detail had to learn was the spotting of targets. We spent days on end just getting our eyes used to seeing anything and everything which might be an enemy position.

"Every man had to learn how to read all kinds of maps so he could locate any spot or route exactly. They also had to learn how to draw maps. We were always doing that at the front—usually with our knees as our drawing boards—and under fire. They could be just crude panoramic sketches but they had to be accurate enough so any position could be recognized and located. During battle, we were building up our panoramic sketches constantly, marking every concentration fired and indicating the nature of the target. After a while, we would have everything located so accurately with relation to our map markings that often we didn't need that second round of adjusting fire.

"The detail had to learn how to read aerial photographs because, often, they are the best possible maps. It isn't as simple as it sounds. Things photographed from twenty thousand feet up don't usually look the same as they do on the ground.

"Then there's communications. Barney knew all about radio but had to learn all about field telephones and how to run wire and keep it in repair. Furman, who knew the telephone inside out, had to learn the radio. Warren and I had to learn both and all of us had to learn wigwag because sometimes all mechanical communications go out and the message still has to get through.

"The telephone is the best and most reliable means of communication both because the enemy can't tune in on it and because it carries voices more distinctly than the radio. Field radios are subject to a lot of interference and they are not as powerful as we would like. So you will do almost anything to keep your telephone lines open, which is why telephone men are so expendable.

"As it is, you have to use the radio a lot. Usually, the forward observer does his radio calling by remote control because it allows him to wander around over quite an area, and have constant communication with his battery or the fire direction center.

"You don't go in for clubby little chats over either the telephone or the radio. All messages are telegraphic and as brief as possible. Over the radio, code is used as much as possible. That made it compulsory for the detail to learn how to handle codes and learn them rapidly because the code generally is changed every day—sometimes two or three times the same day if any one of them is used so much the enemy would have time to decipher it.

"We all had to learn how to·use our voices, too. Messages have to be understood the first time out. There may not be chance for a second time. So a little voice culture was tossed in with the training.

"Since we were going to work with the infantry, we spent a good deal of time with the doughboys, learning something about infantry tactics and infantry weapons, all the way from hand grenades to the cannon.

"We had to learn how to shoot a carbine, too. That's the weapon now issued to all artillery enlisted men instead of the old time forty-five automatic. Officers still get the same old forty-fives, God knows why. But, fortunately—how fortunately I found out later—they must qualify in all weapons used by their outfits.

"All of us had to learn how to keep ourselves as invisible as possible while moving around. That means getting down on your face and learning all the best habits of a snake and how to take advantage of every hill and gully and bush and anything else which can give you defilade. Then there was a little education in the fine art of the shovel, also quick camouflage with whatever is handy. And, naturally, all members of the detail had to learn first aid.

"By the time we went to maneuvers, all of us were tired and the detail had become the most exclusive bunch in the battery. The fellows had a lot of pride in their jobs. They knew they had been hand-picked and they knew they were good. I like that kind of soldier. He never admits anything is impossible. Major Glenn Hubbard, one of our instructors at Fort Sill, used to say, 'People who tell you it can't be done are always being interrupted by somebody doing it.' That detail of ours was always doing it.

"Rick and our assistant executive, Lieutenant Bob Dolan, worked out with us a lot. You see, while the other fellows do have occasional interludes of rest, the forward observer has to be on the job every minute. As it's a strenuous life, he has to be relieved occasionally. The only two officers available for this relief are the battery commander and assistant executive. The relief usually consists of no more than an exchange of jobs, the FO taking over for the man who relieves him. In our detail, for short reliefs of an hour or so, Warren could always take over.

"When we came back from maneuvers, things moved fast. Two weeks later, we were on shipboard, headed for England."

# III

WE MADE A LOT of mistakes in the first few months we were in Africa (said Kennard), not in strategy but in the way the rank and file of us went at things. We should have known better but when it comes to fighting a war, it's a good old American custom to learn the hard way. That's what we did.

When you consider our blunders, though, a lot of things should be remembered which most people have forgotten already, now that our armies are functioning like armies. You have to remember that our armies had to be built from scratch and we didn't start from there until more than a year after Hitler started this war and, before that, nearly 100 per cent of the men now in service never dreamed of becoming soldiers.

You have to remember that for the first year after we did start, late in 1940, we had practically no good camps, no uniforms, not even a fraction of the competent instructors needed for the flood of men who were inducted and we had no weapons. In the artillery, for instance, it is a little hard to become excited if your gun is something whittled out of wood and, to pretend it is firing, somebody has to yell, "Boom!" It wasn't until after Pearl Harbor that we really got under way.

You have to remember they didn't begin to streamline our army for this kind of war until 1940 and it takes time, lots of it, to completely change over the whole military setup of a country as big as ours, and work out all the new angles and put them into operation, especially when our army was growing faster than anybody could keep up with it.

When we landed in Africa, our artillery and infantry and air forces were a long way from being co-ordinated. The commanding generals tried and places like the Field Artillery School at Fort Sill and the Infantry School at Fort Benning hammered away at the necessity for co-ordination and how to bring it about but the idea hadn't seeped in all the way down the line as yet. The old antagonism between the infantry and artillery still was going strong and the air forces felt superior to both of us. In the back of our minds we all knew we could not win this war without complete co-ordination but we still had to learn to put that idea in the front of our minds as the most important thing, instead of just something to think about.

Forward observation needs the closest kind of co-operation with the infantry but it was a long way from that stage when we started in Africa. That was true on the part of both the infantry and the artillery. When we first went into action, we thought we knew our stuff. It took about three days to show we were only in kindergarten. In fact, I proved it so far as I was concerned.

Our combat setup was okay. Ours was one of the new triangular divisions, with three regiments of infantry and three battalions of light field artillery for their direct support. We also had a battalion of the heavier mediums and some reinforcing artillery.

Each regiment of infantry has a battalion of lights in direct support, the two operating as a combat team. The infantry now uses such a variety of weapons, gradually scaling up in size, that there no longer is any gap between the armament of the two branches. Instead of just rifles and machine guns, as in the old days, the doughboys now have Garand semiautomatic rifles, hand grenades, rifle grenades, light and heavy machine guns in both thirty and fifty caliber, antitank guns, light and heavy mortars and each regiment has a platoon of cannon which are something like sawed-off howitzers. The next step from there, of course, is the light field artillery. Naturally, the use of all those weapons has to be co-ordinated perfectly, with each complementing the others.

Speaking of this, Major Hubbard told us one day he felt the time had about come when the infantry and light and medium field artillery no longer should be in separate branches of the service but should be lined up in one branch which might be called just the combat troops. That may be heresy for an artilleryman but, after you've been through the mill, it makes sense.

Everything works in threes in our streamlined triangular divisions. There are three regiments of infantry and three battalions of light artillery. Each artillery battalion has three batteries. Each infantry regiment has three battalions, each battalion has three rifle companies, each rifle company has three rifle platoons and each platoon three rifle squads.

No commander, from the commanding general of an army down to a platoon officer, ever uses all his infantry in action at the same time unless it is absolutely necessary to do so to affect the outcome of the battle. He always tries to keep one third of his infantry force in reserve.

When any unit is assigned to definite action it is said to be "committed." So, in battle, two regiments usually are committed and one is held in reserve. The same policy goes right through the line. In each committed regiment, two battalions are committed, one held in reserve. In each battalion, two rifle companies are committed, one in reserve. Each company has two committed platoons, one reserve, each platoon, two rifle squads committed, one reserve. With that system, when the going gets thick, it doesn't take long to keep on bringing in an extra 50 per cent punch when it's needed.

All that has a great deal to do with forward observation. You see, the reserve idea does not apply to the field artillery. Because, theoretically, its job is supposed to be a little less strenuous than the infantry's, the field artillery keeps right on going, using its full strength all the time.

In battle, each regiment of infantry is assigned to a zone of action which has definite limits on either side. The infantry units which are out in front to carry the load are called the "leading elements." That's a stodgy sort of term but what else are you going to call them in a war in which there is no such thing as a "front line" as there was in the last war? This is a war of movement, so the leading elements are spotted wherever they are in position to do the most good, either to hop off for attack or for defense. So the location of the leading elements is liable to be pretty much of a zigzag, with open gaps between them instead of an unbroken line of soldiers. They cover the gaps with machine-gun and mortar fire.

There is nothing haphazard about the way the doughboys move from these positions, though. When an attack is ordered, a definite "line of departure"—another good two-dollar expression—is fixed all across the zone of attack. That is an imaginary line across which all the doughboys move simultaneously at the exact second set for the attack to begin, called the H hour. The line of departure is usually determined by reference to a road or a fence or some terrain features easy to identify. It isn't always an imaginary line. When General Montgomery started his drive from El Alamein, he didn't have any terrain features to use. He didn't have anything except endless miles of sand. So, shortly before the H hour, his engineers actually laid miles of white tape across the front so the infantry had a line of departure it could see.

All calculations are based upon the line of departure and, because of the usual irregularity of the positions of the leading elements, perfect co-ordination between the doughboys and the artillery is absolutely necessary. We get it by combining direct contact with the infantry and artillery observation.

You see, artillery targets practically never can be seen from the gun positions so there has to be somebody spotted where he can see and adjust fire on them. Each battery has a primary observation post well out in front of the howitzer positions, from which a good deal of the target area can be seen. Then the artillery battalion has a special liaison officer with each infantry battalion. He is with the infantry battalion commander constantly and during action, is with him in the battalion commander's observation post which is farther up front than the battery OP and provides a better view of the target zone.

But these OPs are fixed positions from which many specific parts of the terrain ahead are hidden by hills or other features of the ground. So there has to be somebody else, up far enough and with sufficient freedom of movement to get a complete and unobstructed view, someone who can spot and adjust fire on targets which no one else can see. Also, there must be somebody from the artillery in direct contact with the leading infantry elements, to learn their problems and immediate artillery needs as they develop and get information about targets which the doughboys themselves spot. Also, the artillery wants somebody up there to send back first-hand intelligence information about enemy movements and dispositions, seen either by his own eyes or by infantry patrols and observers.

That's the forward observer. He is all three of those somebodies. He is a sort of roving observation post and contact man. He has only three rules to follow. He must see everything which may be a target, no matter where he has to go to see it, even if he has to sneak up and push a Jerry out of the way to get a look. He must keep in direct contact with the doughboys. He must keep open his communications with his battalion. There's no use learning things if you can't get the information to somebody who can make the right use of it.

In our outfit, when we started in Africa, the zone of action of each of our infantry regiments usually was divided into three zones of observation by the artillery battalion, with one zone assigned to each firing battery. The battery then was responsible for the observation and adjustment of fire on targets in its zone. Each battery had its own forward observer detail which worked the assigned zone. This didn't mean we were confined to the map limits of our zone. We constantly were moving around outside the zone but the purpose was to get a better view of targets which *were* in our own zone.

As soon as our battery went into position, it was up to the FO detail to go up front and get on the job. From there on, we were strictly on our own and practically never saw the battery as long as we were in action. So we had to be self-sufficient. We had our own jeep, carried our own rations, weapons, ammunition, blanket rolls, ran our own telephone lines and kept them in repair and, of course, carried our own radio set. Naturally, the jeep had to be parked out of sight quite a distance behind our forward positions and, from there, we carried everything by hand. The radio gave us the most grief in that line. The artillery field radio set is put up in two cases—about the size of suitcases—and heavy. To use the radio, the two cases are clamped together. A remote control phone is attached to the set with as many hundred yards of extension cable as the forward observer needs in moving around. We carried our own shovels, too, and we kept them handy. You do a lot of digging in this war—and at very high speed. When hot stuff begins falling around you, there's nothing so beautiful as a nice, deep hole. Many's the time I've thought the shovel was God's greatest inspiration to man.

Still, forward observing is really the prime job of the army. All you have to do is look, listen and talk. You don't even have to say much. You have all the modern conveniences —automobile, telephone, radio. And then, there's the freedom of it—just you and the fellows of the detail, all alone up there in God's great outdoors, with nobody to boss you around. And the working conditions are wonderful—no time

clock to punch, no union dues to pay, no worry about over-
time. The hours are just from daylight until the war is over.

You have the right to knock off and go to sleep any time
you have the chance. Sometimes you have a chance on Tues-
day and then you have another chance on Friday and, if
everything goes right, you may not have to wait longer than
till Sunday for another snooze. Yes, sir. It's the life.

Just the same, I'd rather be a forward observer than anything else in the army. It's always interesting and exciting
but, more than that, there's a lot of satisfaction in it. You see
the results of your work unfold before your eyes all the time
and every time you lay your howitzers on a target—well, you
know that's one more thing out of the way on the road to the
end of the war.

I was taking the Battery Officers Course at Fort Sill when
I decided that forward observing was for me. Maybe it was
the way Major Hubbard presented it and the way Captain
Paul Callahan * put us through the ropes out on the range.
Anyway, I fell for it.

It was Rick Hallon who finally swung it for me. Maybe it
wouldn't have made any difference but sometimes I wonder
if it wasn't the biggest mistake he ever made—for him—not
for me.

* Now Major Callahan.

# IV

WHILE WE WERE in England, we kept right on training, trying to polish the rough spots as best we could. There wasn't much formality about the detail. We all knew each other's jobs and pitched in together on anything that involved the detail, so rank didn't mean much. Reminds me of another of Major Hubbard's cracks when he said the way this war was going it was getting so an officer even had to know what an enlisted man does.

Actually, we weren't in England very long. Almost before we knew it, we were aboard ship again as part of that big convoy to Africa. And, almost the minute we set foot on shore, we found ourselves fighting. Some American outfits had a much tougher time of it than we did but it was bad enough where we were. The French put up an almost ferocious fight at first. The whole thing seemed all wrong, a rough and tumble show that cost lives and was entirely unnecessary. We hadn't come over to fight the French and we were mighty glad when their Vichy commanders surrendered. So were most of the French soldiers, judging by the way they came flocking to our side.

After that we had a short breather while we really were getting organized on shore, though we didn't have time to see much of the country. Almost as soon as we were set, we were ordered east.

We can't tell you much about the grand strategy and the broad tactical maneuvers of the Tunisian campaign. We were through it all the way but nobody knows as little about a battle as the men who are in it. All we actually saw of it was what happened right around us. That kept us so busy we didn't have time even to ask about the rest of it.

When we started, all we knew was that General Eisenhower was trying to reach Tunis and Bizerte before the Axis had time to bring in enough reinforcements to stop us. We would have made it, too, if it hadn't been for the unspeakable weather we ran into and the way we had to stretch our supply lines so fast and so far over country which didn't have enough roads to maintain a division, to say nothing of a couple of armies.

The FO jeep was all spick and span and packed very neatly the day we started. It didn't stay pretty long, although it always had to be packed right because of the amount of stuff we had to carry. Even with perfect packing only three men can ride in the FO jeep. The instrument corporal drives, the RO rides with him in the front seat and the radio operator squeezes in the back with the equipment. That makes it necessary for the telephone man to ride on the battery wire truck but that works out all right. It keeps him posted on the battery telephone lines and makes it easier and quicker for him to hook the FO line to the battery wire head when we're in the field.

So it was Warren and Johns and myself in the jeep. As we went along, we heard plenty of rumors about meeting opposition in Algeria but nothing happened. It was a good deal like a long training hike.

We were very sure of ourselves—too sure. Nothing could stop us. We knew everything about how to smash the Nazis. Besides, we were Americans, which automatically gave us two strikes on every other gang in the world. That's how most of us felt. The trouble was too many seemed to think Americans had some special kind of body which couldn't be damaged by Nazi ammunition so they didn't bother much to protect themselves as they had been taught. By the time they learned it only takes one slug from anybody's gun to kill a man, it was too late for the education to do them much good. Sure, it's tiresome and a damned nuisance to dig a hole for yourself every time you stop for five or ten minutes but it's a lot more fun being tired and alive than rested and dead. Our real education began the morning we crossed the border into Tunisia. Since we were heading into certain combat which might start any time, our vehicles were spread out according to Hoyle—a hundred to a hundred and fifty yards apart, so any one bomb couldn't knock out more than one truck and one truck isn't a very profitable target for one bomb when you consider all the trouble it takes to bring the bomb there.

It was about ten o'clock when the first air alarm came from the head of the column, miles up front, announcing enemy planes headed our way. That meant get off the road quick and head for anything that looked like cover, then scramble away from the vehicle. Every truck in the column made a break to one side or the other but a lot of them still were in motion when the planes peeled off and swooped down on the column, dropping their eggs as they dived.

Warren drove the jeep into a patch of woods to the right of the road and we had just time to jump out when the first plane went by, ripping at everything in sight. Every anti-aircraft gun in the column was throwing lead into the air and making a lot of racket but none of the planes even slowed down.

There was a double explosion down the line and when the smoke cleared, we could see one of our trucks burning. When the sound of exploding bombs died away, we took a look from the edge of the trees and then ducked right back. The Jerries weren't leaving us. They zoomed up, circled and came back, this time blazing away with their machine guns.

One of them dived our way and strafed our hide-out, just on general principles, I suppose. He came so low, Jack and Barney were popping at him with their carbines and I was firing my automatic. That day I first began to inkle what a silly combat weapon it is. The Jerry didn't hit anything but neither did we and we didn't care much for a tie score. Through the whole business we felt like fish in a barrel and we didn't like it.

Our machine guns still were going at top speed and the only consolation we had was that one of the planes was damaged and was wobbling as it pulled out of the fight.

When we came up for air, we found the battery had lost just the one truck and there had been no one in it. One man had had his leg gashed by a bomb splinter but all he needed was a little first aid. Farther up the line, we could see half a dozen trucks burning and we heard there had been a number of casualties.

We were under way again in about ten minutes but our necks began to stiffen from keeping our faces toward the sky. All at once, we were very airplane conscious, especially conscious that we had not seen one of our own all morning and we wondered why.

We were still wondering about noon when the Jerries came back and brought some friends and relatives with them. We had our alarm a bit earlier this time and we broke off the road faster but the strafing was much worse than we'd had in the morning. The country was absolutely open. There wasn't a sign of anything that might give us protection. Warren headed straight off the road at a right angle, giving the jeep everything it would take. We were a good two hundred yards over when the rattle of machine guns told us trouble had arrived. We stopped where we were, jumped out and scattered.

All we could do was flatten out with our faces in the dirt and pray for luck. Looking up at a time like that is very unhealthy so we didn't see the plane swoop down directly over us but we heard it. It sounded so low we thought it was going to scrape us off the ground and, for the first time, we heard that nasty hist! a machine-gun bullet makes on its way past your ear. The best thing about that was that we heard it, which meant it had missed.

The racket was terrific. Machine guns were going and bombs were dropping but we kept our heads down. It seemed an endless time before the roar of the airplane motors began to fade and we knew this session was over.

When I stood up and headed for the jeep, the first thing I heard was Warren using a lot of two-dollar cuss words. He was trotting toward our buggy and pointing at the wheels. Neither he nor Johns had been hurt but the Heinie had given us two flat tires. There were half a dozen bullet scars on the body of the car, too.

We could see some fires up ahead and one or two behind us which meant more trucks had taken a beating but our battery hadn't lost any this time. Then, and for the rest of the African campaign, we became known as the "lucky" battery because, in normal action our casualties always seemed lighter than those of other outfits. But it wasn't luck. In six months of combat, I've seen quite a number of those so-called "lucky" outfits but their only luck was having commanders who knew how to make their men take every possible precaution. Rick was one of those. He never let up on the subject. Once, a month later, one of the battery corporals exposed himself unnecessarily. He was really lucky. A shell splinter knocked off his helmet and he was only stunned. Rick busted him on the spot and said anybody else caught violating the security rules would be hauled before a summary court.

In this second strafing we had one man killed—our only casualty—because he was tired of keeping his head down. When he raised himself on one arm to see what was going on, he was hit by a bomb splinter which wouldn't have touched him if he'd stayed flat. Rick felt badly about it, practically deciding it was his fault because one of his men hadn't had sense enough to obey orders.

When we finally were under way again, there was a good deal of grumbling because our own fliers seemed to be letting the Jerries have a Roman holiday at our expense, but there wasn't time to explain to every man in the column that our air forces were just beginning to organize captured airfields and that, at that time, practically all of our air support still was carrier based. What bothered us most was that the strafings indicated the enemy already had a lot of planes in Tunisia, which meant they probably had a lot of other stuff, too.

It was about fifteen hundred—three o'clock—when they came back for the third time. We were in hilly country now and managed to get our jeep into fair defilade. When we jumped out, Warren said, "This is getting monotonous. A little more of it and we'll be in a rut."

A lot of things were different this time, though. I guess the gang which had hit us before had spread the word there was nothing to fear from our flak, so this crowd came in low, almost as if they were contemptuous of us, which was a mistake. We may be a little ignorant when we start but we learn fast. This time, our machine guns began to concentrate their fire. The first plane swooped by without being hurt but the second took a full load of our fire. It worked. The plane zoomed almost straight up, wobbled as if it were off balance when it straightened out and began stumbling away like a drunken sailor.

Another went by but the fourth sailed straight into all the machine guns could pitch. The airplanes used in this war can collect a lot of lead and still keep flying but our fire must have hit something vital in this one. Its momentum carried it past us, then it seemed almost to stop in midair. Next, it jumped about a hundred feet and a heavy trail of smoke poured from it. The pilot nosed straight up, leveled and swung away to the right of our column, then zoomed up again. There was a terrific explosion and, after that, the plane just wasn't there any more and parts of it were showering all over the landscape.

You could have heard our yell all over Tunisia. The whole thing must have been a shock to the other Jerry planes. All of them climbed, circled for a couple of minutes, then headed for home.

That was our real introduction to the war for which we had come to Africa.

# V

AFTER THAT we traveled at night and bivouacked during the day under cover of the olive groves but the strafings became an accepted part of each day's troubles. At that time, the Axis had a definite edge on us in the air and it was quite a while before we caught up. After that first day, the planes we did have were on the job, giving the Jerries strafing for strafing. The curious part of it was that through most of the Tunisian campaign, the strafings seemed to be on a turn and turnabout basis. Our fliers would go by overhead to bomb and strafe the Jerry ground troops. Then, just about the time ours were back at their airfields, the Jerries would come over and hand the same thing to us. By the time our planes were refueled and had a new load of ammunition, the Jerries would have done their stuff and be gone. This just went on and on. We never saw a dogfight on those regular strafing runs.

Between the strafings we just kept going east until the day finally came when Rick was called up to see the battalion commander. When he came back he said we were near the end of the line and would move on immediately. A considerable enemy force was reported heading west not too far ahead of us. A couple of French units were up front, doing their best, with their limited equipment, to hold the advance enemy units until we could come up.

It was early afternoon when we first heard the low, muffled rumbling in the distance and we knew it wasn't thunder. You could feel the tension which suddenly gripped the whole column and you could almost see the efforts the drivers were making to hold down their speed.

The rumbling gradually became louder as we moved forward, subsided almost entirely for a while then started again, louder than before. Squadrons of our fighters and bombers roared overhead, straight for the gunfire. In the distance, we could see them peel off and from the roar which came back, we knew the bombers were dropping their eggs on something behind the hills. Shortly after that, the column was halted and the orders came to leave the road and take cover.

A little later, Rick called me. The firing up ahead had died to a whisper—just a lonesome shot once in a while. Rick said our combat team, that is, our battalion and the infantry regiment we were supporting would deploy to the right and would move into position for business that night, taking over the extreme right flank.

In Rick's jeep, he, Lieutenant Barrett, our battery "exec," and I headed across country. It was about sixteen hundred—four o'clock—when a route marker flagged us down, telling us this was as far as we could go in the car. So we parked it in a wadi and went ahead on foot.

We moved up through the rear echelon of the French, which was about the skimpiest I've ever seen. Their supply dumps were pathetic and conditions didn't improve when we reached their gun positions. For artillery, all they had was a few 1917 seventy-fives and 1917 ammunition and their infantry wasn't equipped much better. I'll hand it to those Frenchmen. They didn't think they had a prayer when they moved in—just a handful of them with a handful of artillery and not much more than a handful of ammunition. But they had done a swell job. They even had trapped one oversized Nazi patrol in a narrow pass and poured enough shrapnel on it to make it give up. Shrapnel! It has been so long since shrapnel has been used in combat that, believe it or not, when the Nazi officer surrendered, he asked to see the new weapon the French had been using on him. But most of those Frenchmen had families in occupied France. When they had a new chance at the Nazis, their hearts were in it. So they just trusted to guts and God and got away with it.

This day, things had been tough for them. They did the best they could with their museum pieces but their ammunition was running out. More Jerries had shown up, too, and were pushing them back when our planes had saved the situation, handing the Jerries such a pasting they had to abandon their advanced positions. But the French had had neither the strength nor the ammunition to follow them up.

When we moved up to the irregular rise behind which the French infantry had taken their position, smoke still was rising from the wreckage of enemy matériel our bombers had blasted down in front of us but nothing else was happening. We were told the Jerries had retired behind a ridge about four thousand yards ahead of us. It looked like a good defensive position. From the ridge, two irregular series of smaller hills extended toward us for about a thousand yards. One row of hills marked the extreme right of the combat zone. The other was roughly six hundred yards to the left. Between them was a sort of wide valley of rolling ground leading to the ridge.

The whole combat area extended for miles to the left. The French had been able to hold fairly well all along the line because the enemy forces still were comparatively light. Our job was to drive them back before they could be strengthened by the troops we had been told were coming up.

Our battalion commander, the colonel of our infantry regiment and the French commander were in a huddle when we came up, checking maps and looking at the terrain ahead through their binoculars. The Frenchman did a good deal of pointing at the flanking hills. It seemed almost impossible to believe we were in a combat zone. There were occasional bursts of firing off to our left but it was absolutely quiet where we were.

When the conference broke up and Rick reported, our

battalion commander said we were going to move in after dark and attack at daybreak. The heaviest enemy concentration was reported to be a couple of miles to our left. The tanks we had available were going to spearhead the drive there. The particular job of our combat team was to hit hard and fast and turn the Jerries' flank. During the night, our doughboys were going to move in well beyond the French positions with our battalion right behind them. Our battery zone of observation was to be the six-hundred-yard stretch between the rows of hills. The line of departure in our zone was to be a short distance this side of the nearest hills.

The three of us—Rick, Barrett and I—started forward. Up to the place we chose for the battery position, the going was fairly easy with plenty of defilade to shield us. Rick and Barrett staked out the howitzer emplacements, then Rick and I went on ahead. Some distance up, he tagged a rise for his primary observation post and then we reconnoitered the area ahead. There were exposed stretches up here and that was where we started our grand tour of Tunisia on our hands and knees. We crawled over rocks and through brush about half the time, stopping whenever we thought we had a good place to look and trying to spot targets on the hills which were naturals for machine gun and mortar emplacements. The French already had reported some of these and we were lucky enough to sight some more which we charted for artillery attention. We also spotted possible observation posts for the FO detail and a place to park the jeep when we came up that night.

It was nearly dark when we reached our outfit again and the whole battalion was getting ready to move up fast. After Rick and I had some chow together, I joined the FO detail which was all set and raring to go.

The sky had become heavily overcast late in the afternoon and it was pitch dark when we finally started, depending upon the car just ahead of us to keep us going right. After dark at the front, the open order traffic is out. Trucks follow each other as closely as they can, to avoid losing their way and route markers are stationed at intervals all along the way to keep them headed right.

When we reached the battery position, excitement was pounding through everybody. We had mixed it a little with the French when we first landed and we had been under fire from the air but this was the first time we were going in to do the real job for which we had been trained. But everything was under control. Digging emplacements and rigging up camouflage is no picnic in the dark and we were within easy range of enemy artillery but the fellows went at the job as smoothly as if they were just on maneuvers. While they were at that, we started our own job.

The routine we went through that day and night is the one an FO detail always must follow in a new combat zone.

We parked our jeep near the primary OP then made a complete check of our equipment to be sure we had everything we needed, especially rations and water. My final duty before going up was to check with Rick. I did this as soon as he came back from the conference with the battalion commander at which the complete attack plans were explained.

Rick and I squatted on the ground under a blanket with a flashlight and went over the maps. From Rick I had to learn the exact time of the H hour, the exact map location of the line of departure, of our base point, of each battery, of the battalion's fire direction center, of all the command posts —that of our battalion commander, the infantry regimental commander, the infantry battalion commanders—of the infantry battalion observation posts, since our liaison officers would be there, also the location of the reinforcing artillery, the mediums and the leading infantry elements. I had to learn from him the complete plan of communications for the battalion, where our battery wire head would be so we could hook up to it without losing time, how much ammunition we had and what kind, the code to be used the next day, what the infantry rocket signals would be if any were needed, the complete plan of attack, the succession of objectives and the time each was supposed to be reached.

All this had to be memorized because none of this information may be marked on any maps taken to the forward zones. If a forward observer is captured—and there's always that chance—his maps must give the enemy no information about the location and disposition of his own forces.

Then I had to get from Rick the complete plan of artillery fires for the battalion. By this time, through information from the French, our own reconnaissance and that of the other forward observers and our liaison officers and first reports from infantry patrols, a lot of targets had been charted and given concentration numbers. These could be marked on the maps we were taking with us. The targets were all in enemy territory and, if the maps were captured, they would be telling nothing the enemy didn't know already.

Rick said there was to be no advance artillery preparation. We were hoping for the surprise element in the attack so our howitzers would not open up until the doughboys crossed the line of departure. At that time, though, our zone was to have priority on fire to smash the enemy emplacements on the hills which flanked the line of attack. Since our objective was to turn the enemy flank, the main effort naturally would be made on our side and an entire infantry battalion was assigned to the job, with the other committed battalion spread over the rest of the regimental zone of action to our left. This meant there would be two committed rifle companies in our zone, with the one on the right carrying the load. It was to move forward as rapidly as possible along the hills on the right. The left company was to mop up the Jerries on the hills at the left after the artillery finished its job.

Rick recommended that we contact the right company

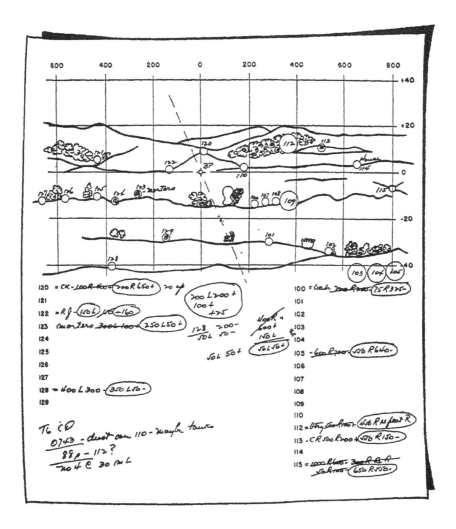

The Forward Observer drew this panoramic sketch of enemy territory during action. Vertical lines mark distance in yards to right and left of Base Point ("BP" in center of sketch). Horizontal lines are guides to elevations of targets with reference to the Base Point. Circles indicate targets with concentration numbers assigned to them for easy reference. Large circles are, previously marked targets upon which adjusted concentrations have been fired, providing an accurate key to terrain distances and fire adjustment on other targets. Small circles mark new targets spotted by the Forward Observer. His computations and notes on the targets are written below the sketch.

and stay with it. He said he would arrange through our liaison officer to have the left company keep in touch with us.

When we finally tossed aside the blanket and stood up, we shook hands. After all, this was going to be our first real battle and I guess we were a little sober about it.

The detail was standing by at the jeep and all four of us went through the blanket and flashlight routine while I passed on all the information Rick had given me. A forward observer always does this. It's mighty important for every member of the detail to know what the score is all the time. It saves a lot of orders. Besides, you never can tell when any one of them may have to take over the whole job.

When we doused the light and I said, "All right, let's go," Warren and Johns shook hands solemnly with Furman who was coming up on the battery wire truck, of course. They said good-by to him with a catch in their voices and told him they hoped he, too, would get into the war some time. Then we hopped into our buggy and were on our way.

*

# VI

WE HAD A ROUGH TRIP, bouncing around in the dark, scarcely able to see half a dozen feet in front of the car. We ran through some doughboy reserves who barked at us to "get that damned target away from there" which we were doing as fast as we could. We almost missed the defilade where we were going to park the jeep but finally found it and ran it among the rocks and brush.

Warren and I climbed out and started forward. It was Barney's job to give the jeep what camouflage he could in the dark, watch for the battery wire truck and get Furman's wire over to him to save time in connecting our telephone line with the battery's. As an extra precaution against tipping our movements or position, radio silence had been ordered until the attack began, so there was no use in our taking up the radio set until we knew where we were going to put it.

Warren and I hadn't gone far before we were challenged by one of the infantry guides staked out for just such wanderers as ourselves. He directed us toward the infantry company we were hunting and we practically stumbled over the rise we wanted to use for our first observation point. Fifty yards beyond it we found the doughboy captain and a couple of his lieutenants sitting on the edges of their foxholes, talking things over. I introduced Warren and myself to the captain and we got off to a great start.

He said he was glad the artillery was going to have *somebody* up there. He scarcely listened when I told him the general positions of the batteries. I told him where we were going to be and that didn't seem to interest him either. His attitude was, "So what?" After a good deal of coaxing, he showed us on the map by flashlight under my raincoat where the other leading elements were, grudgingly, almost suspiciously. When I indicated the concentrations we were going to fire and told him of our priority on the hills which flanked the zone, he said it was just a waste of ammunition because there were no Jerries on the hills. He said he had made the reconnaissance personally just before dark and hadn't seen a sign of life.

He said he hoped our howitzers wouldn't knock off too many of his men when they started. It took a little effort but I held my temper and told him he needn't worry if he took his men where they were supposed to go at the time scheduled. He said that, offhand, he didn't know of any new targets for us but he had some patrols out and if they brought in anything he thought we ought to know he would pass it along.

While we still were looking at the map, he said, belligerently, "You're not marking on the map the positions of our outfits, are you?" I told him I had a bad cramp in my map-marking hand so I'd try to memorize what he had told me. He wanted to know if we were observing radio silence. He said he didn't want any artillery radio giving away any position at which the Jerries could shoot and have the shorts killing some of his men. When I asked him if it were okay for me to have our observation point where I had indicated, he looked at me as if he thought I were kidding.

He was a long way from being typical of infantry officers. He was just a hang-over from the feud days and turned out to be a rare exception, especially after the first few days.

As soon as we were back in our own position, I wrote Rick a note, giving him our exact location and the dope the captain had passed out. Warren took it to the battery wire corporal at the wire head to deliver to Rick as the information had to go through as soon as possible and we had no other means of communication as yet.

After he left I started digging. We still were using the

old standard artillery slit trenches then instead of the dough-boy foxholes we came around to before long. Slit trenches are long and just deep enough so a man can stretch out in them below ground level. They're okay against machine-gun fire and artillery shells which burst on impact but they are plain murder under air strafing, bombs and time fused or ricochet artillery projectiles which burst above ground. They're worse than murder under rolling tanks. We had to learn that by experience, too. Foxholes are vertical, shoulder deep, with the opening just big enough to squeeze through, but wider at the bottom, so you can crouch down in them with your head below ground level. That way, nothing but a direct hit can touch you.

So I dug me a very swell slit trench, started one each for Furman and Warren, quite a distance apart, and had just dropped down the rise and begun a hole for Johns and the radio set which always must be dug in as deeply as possible, when Barney and Warren showed up, carrying the set. Certainly I did my own digging. The other fellows were busy, we had a heavy day ahead of us and, if any of us were to have any rest, we all had to do whatever we could to get things ready.

As soon as he deposited his half of the set, Barney went back to service the telephone line Furman was running from the battery wire head. Servicing a line just means giving it as much protection as possible and making sure it isn't taut anywhere because a taut wire is duck soup for concussion. Warren and I kept on digging until Furman came in, attached the telephone instrument to the line and checked it through to make sure it was okay. Barney hadn't had much of a servicing job and came in a few minutes later.

I called Rick and told him we would keep the telephone line open, with one man on it all the time. It was nearly midnight before we were all set, trenches finished and radio set dug in. Warren went on the first watch from midnight to two, with Barney going on from two to four and Furman from four to six by which time we all were going to be awake.

Since I hadn't heard from the doughboy captain, I told the fellows to wake me as soon as any message came from him. If none came, Furman was to wake me at four o'clock so I could go up for a final huddle with the captain.

It was Warren who awoke me. Toward the end of his watch, he had heard movement up ahead and, on a hunch, had gone up to investigate as soon as Barney relieved him. Twenty minutes after that he was back shaking me.

"Lieutenant," he said as soon as I was conscious, "the doughboys are gone!"

It didn't make sense but he was in dead earnest and when we scrambled out to where we had seen the captain, there was no sign of him or anybody else. Jack said he already had gone quite a distance beyond without finding anything. I began to feel a little dizzy. It just wasn't possible that my clubby captain and his company had vanished. Only they weren't there. The only thing I could figure was that there had been a sudden change in plans, relocating the leading elements and a slip-up on notifying us.

We hustled back and I called Rick. He was flabbergasted, said he knew nothing about any change in plans but he would find out quick and, meanwhile, we had better try to find the missing infantry. So Warren and I started out again. We crossed the line of departure and then kept going and had stumbled and crawled several hundred yards when who should loom up but our friend, the guide. He said, sure, they had moved up and were just ahead of us.

It was another good hundred yards before we reached the captain. Apparently, the whole company had just arrived. We could hear them digging all around us and the captain himself had just been handed his newly connected telephone when we came up. He had just said "Major Barlow" into the phone when he saw us. He looked at us out of the corner of his eyes and said, "Oh, it's you," a little on the sour side and then started talking over the phone. It was a speech I'll never forget.

"Major Barlow," he said and you could almost hear his chest bulging with pride, "our patrols found no sign of the enemy for more than six hundred yards ahead of us so I took advantage of the opportunity to improve our attack position by advancing the company that much further. I did this before notifying you because I wished to be established in our new positions while it was still dark. . . . What was that, sir? . . . I beg your pardon, sir. . . . It was my best judgment, sir. . . . Yes, sir. . . . Yes, sir. . . . Y-e-s, s-i-r."

His chest had gone concave by the time he hung up. He growled to his top sergeant, "Move the company back to where we were—and make it snappy." The topper gave him a funny look as he moved away and when he issued the order, we could hear the whole company griping. No wonder. They had been robbed of a lot of sleep with a tough day ahead. The captain told the telephone man to keep the line open, then turned to us and barked, "What do you want?"

"Nothing now, sir," I said. "It's just part of our job to keep in touch with the infantry unit nearest us. So when we discovered you had gone without notifying us, we had to look for you."

"You could have saved yourself the trouble," he growled. "I thought the idea of this fight was to advance."

"If you can do it without being killed," I said.

"Not a shot has been fired," he came back.

"There would be first thing in the morning," I said. "You are completely enfiladed by machine guns and mortars on the hills on both sides of you here."

"I told you there wasn't anything on those hills," he snapped and just then, one of his patrols came up and said they'd scouted the near-by hills and spotted two machine-gun nests and a mortar emplacement and there probably were more but they had to duck to avoid being captured.

The captain just stood there with his mouth open. Then the telephone man said, "Major Barlow calling the captain, sir."

I guess the captain knew he wasn't going to like what was coming. He pressed the receiver so tightly to his ear not a word leaked out. After he had been listening for a while he said, in a surprised way, "Now, sir?" and then with his voice in his shoes, "Yes, sir."

He looked a little dazed when he handed the telephone back to the operator. He turned to the first lieutenant who was standing near and said, "Take over. I've been called to headquarters." Then, without another look at any of us, he started back in a hurry.

The lieutenant looked at me and shrugged his shoulders. "I have a hunch you'll be working with me today," he said in a dry sort of voice.

Before either of us could say anything else, another of the doughboys came hurrying up. He said he had been scouting up the valley and had just escaped being caught by what looked like several machine-gun crews with their weapons coming our way. One of the second lieutenants said, "We can let them walk right into us and fold 'em up."

"And have every machine gun on those hills open up on us," the first lieutenant said. "No, we'll beat it back before they find out we're around. Get going."

He turned to me and said, "My name's Byrnes—Bill Byrnes. I know you're Kennard. Want to talk things over on the way back?" He told the scout who had seen the machine-gun crews coming to stick around until he knew exactly where they located then to hustle back and report. "Lieutenant Kennard will want the dope so the artillery can take care of 'em," he said.

"This," I said to myself, "is a guy I'm going to like."

On the way back he said he'd done everything but knock the captain down to keep him from shooing the company forward. "I knew it was crazy and told him so," Byrnes said. "He usually has more sense, too. Must be battle jitters. He's been on edge ever since we came up."

It took about three minutes to learn he considered the field artillery the doughboys' best friend in time of trouble and, after that, we were bosom pals. By the time we reached the original company position, he had given me a lot of valuable information and I had the map location of the emplacements the patrol found on the hills. Then the other scout came in to report where the Jerry machine gunners had planted themselves. Meanwhile, Byrnes had sent out another patrol to look over the hills on the right and it brought back more target information. So I had a lot of new data for Rick when I reached my own telephone again, stepping up the number of concentrations we had to fire in our zone.

We never saw the captain again. Later, word drifted up that, after Major Barlow, the infantry battalion commander, had taken him apart, the colonel did an even better job and then sent him back with the recommendation that he be assigned to some post where he couldn't kill anybody. It was lucky all around, except for the captain. An unreliable officer had been spotted before he could do any damage and the company went into the hands of a man who seemed to know his stuff.

While I was huddling with Byrnes again, a runner came from the left company with word that one of its patrols had spotted another enemy machine-gun position being set up about three hundred yards to the left of the first one on the floor of the valley. He also brought information that the Jerries had scattered machine-gun and mortar positions all along the hills up to the ridge. He had their exact locations, which helped a lot. Then another of Byrnes' patrols came in. It had circled back of the advanced enemy machine-guns on the right and had seen still another contingent setting up a mortar position in the valley. Meanwhile, the left company sent over the location of new targets spotted on the hills on its side.

By the time we had charted all the new target positions, our maps looked as if they were decorated with chains of interlocking circles for the concentrations. When I called Rick and gave him all the dope, he whistled and told me to stand by for new orders.

About half an hour later, they came. Because the enemy had established a setup which promised plenty of trouble for anybody attacking up the valley, our battalion would start firing at H minus fifteen—that is, fifteen minutes before the actual time of the attack. Since none of the enemy positions was very elaborate, the howitzers wouldn't spend much time on any one target. The plan was to plaster the positions on the forward hills on each side, next knock off those set up in the valley during the night, then rake the hills with fire all the way to the ridge.

"It won't be very light when we start," Rick said. "You will be able to see better than we can back here. It's all yours."

We were to start with concentration 112, the forward hill on the left, which was the nearest target and so well charted we were opening up with a battalion salvo.

All the fellows in the detail were awake by now, so we had breakfast of C rations and water. After that, we checked everything again to make sure we were set and eased into our trenches. I told Furman he might as well crawl down behind Barney and get some rest while he could since—we hoped— he wouldn't be working for a while but he said, "Do you mind if I stay here and watch, sir?" so he stretched out in his slit trench. Barney raised a howl because he had to stay down in his hole with the radio and couldn't see what was going on. All of us were pretty well keyed up. It *was* our first battle and we were going to direct the first act.

We started looking at our watches every few seconds. It was five minutes to go, then four, then three, two, one. The landscape had turned from black to gray and looked mighty bleak under the heavy clouds which still covered the sky but, up ahead, things gradually were taking tangible form. We could see the hills distinctly now and the doughboys in their foxholes just ahead of us. Through my binoculars I thought I even could see the camouflaged enemy machine-gun and mortar positions up the valley.

Then Rick came on the telephone saying, "All set?" and I answered, "All set." The S-3 * at the fire direction center came on and said, "Stand by." I watched the second hand of my watch move around. As it reached sixty, the S-3's voice came again, "On the way," and every howitzer in the battalion let go.

* Officer in charge of battalion operations.

# VII

WE HAD TO LEARN a lot of things in Africa, but gunnery wasn't one of them. There never was anything wrong with the marksmanship of American gun crews or the speed with which they shifted from one target to another. That first battalion volley was right on.

It affected us as nothing else had so far. When we saw those twelve shells smashing into a live target, for the first time it hit us with a bang that we actually were on the job in this war. For the first time, too, we were struck by the size of our responsibility to the doughboys in front of us and the gun crews behind us. But we only had a second for that. There was too much to do.

When twelve one-o-five projectiles all hit about the same spot, it doesn't take many rounds to smash a machine-gun nest. After two, I could say, "Mission accomplished. Up two hundred," and after two more rounds, "Up two hundred again."

Just then Warren yelled and pointed to the forward hill on the right. We could see small puffs of smoke coming from it and then heard the zip of machine-gun bullets over our heads. Down in front of us, a doughboy, a little previous in climbing out of his foxhole, jerked upright and toppled over, the first man hit.

I called for fire on the hill. In twenty seconds, the adjusting battery salvo came over, about a hundred yards short and another hundred to the right. It took the battalion about fifteen seconds to fix that and the next volley was for effect. It was effective. The machine-gun fire stopped on the second battalion round and then it was the doughboys who yelled.

After stretching the range twice on that side to take care of enemy positions beyond the first one, we went to work on the three positions in the valley. I remember the thing that kept drumming through my mind most was that we were getting the targets on the second round every time, according to Fort Sill standards. Most of the Jerries in those three valley positions were killed or wounded. Not a shot ever was fired from them. When our fire lifted, we could see a few men scrambling away from them back toward the ridge but they were very few.

After that, the battalion went on the job of giving the hills on both sides of the valley a complete going over. Directing fire was easy, a battery salvo for adjustment, then "Fire for effect," a couple of battalion volleys, extend the range, change the deflection and fire for effect again. Most of the time, the adjusting salvo wasn't necessary.

We were still at it when my watch showed just thirty seconds before H hour. Down in front of us, all the doughboys were climbing out of their foxholes. Byrnes moved out in front of them. He looked back toward us and waved, then gave the arm signal for forward and they were on their way. Over on the left, I could see the other company also heading for the line of departure.

Just as they crossed it, every piece of artillery we had on that front opened up with such a blast the whole landscape seemed to jump. Up to that time, our battalion had been playing solo. Now it became just part of a heavy chorus. Their immediate job for us was finished so our "hows" shifted to the other zones for a while but the mediums began playing a tune on the ridge up ahead and, after a while, our battalion came back to join in and we went to work again.

The preliminary fire on the hills had been so effective that the doughboys assigned to mopping up didn't have much to do and had no trouble keeping pace with the men moving up the valley itself. They seemed to be having a walk through and were going ahead so fast, we had to leave our position and move up to keep in touch with them.

Just before we left, enemy artillery began dropping shells in our zone for the first time. They were overshooting the doughboys by several hundred yards but gradually began shortening their range and, at the same time, pouring in heavier fire. Rick told me there had been a lot of difficulty locating the enemy batteries and asked if we could spot any place from which the rear echelons of the Jerries could be observed. I told him there was a peak up ahead on the right which seemed to command a view through a gap in the ridge and we would try it.

We had picked a rise away up for our next observation point and Furman started running his wire toward it with Warren going along while Barney and I packed the radio set up the peak. We had just reached the top when the Jerry artillery caught up with our doughboys and we could see them duck for cover. But we had been lucky. Our peak gave us a swell view of the country behind the ridge and we saw a lot of muzzle flashes that meant battery positions back there.

As soon as Barney had his radio set up behind some rocks, I reported the layout. The S-3 came back almost immediately to say the mediums would take on the counter-battery fire and to send in the missions. The angle from which we were observing was a tough one and I admit, with head bowed, that I needed three adjusting rounds to get on the first Jerry battery.

The mediums were just going to town when we heard another sound overhead and looked up to see a flock of enemy planes peeling out of formation and diving for the doughboys in our zone. Between the artillery fire which we hadn't slowed down yet and the bombing and machine-gunning from the air they seemed to be taking a heavy beating. I had to keep my eyes on the battery targets for the mediums and couldn't watch what was happening anywhere else but, just when I was beginning to develop another gripe about the absence of our own planes, a bunch of them dropped out of the clouds.

The mediums really were hashing up those enemy batteries one by one, so I had to keep on directing fire but Barney told me the dogfight was swell while it lasted. I sneaked one quick look up and saw three swastika-marked planes coming down in flames at the same time—a very gorgeous sight.

By this time, I could see only one gun still firing in the three batteries the mediums already had socked and the fire on the doughboys was letting up a little. It let up some more when the mediums sprayed the other two batteries we could see from our perch. While they were on the fourth one, I looked upstairs again. Another Jerry was dropping but so was one of our planes. It crashed just below us but there was nothing we could do. You can't be a human being in war. Maybe we could have reached the plane and pulled out the pilot before the flames got to him. We'll never know. We had to stay on the job we were doing. Maybe more lives were saved by silencing those enemy batteries but that didn't make it any easier to watch one of our own pilots burn to death without being able to lift a hand for him.

By the time the last mission on those batteries was accomplished, the enemy planes which were left had headed for home, the Jerry artillery fire was down to a whisper and our doughboys were starting forward again. We grabbed the radio cases and scrambled down hill.

When we reached our new observation point, Furman already had the telephone line in and Warren was in a shell hole directing a fire mission on a machine-gun position which had been giving Byrnes enough trouble to hold him up. Warren had the hows on the target and the company was moving again. It kept on going until it took cover at the base of the ridge for a breather before the assault. We moved again, too, up alongside Byrnes.

A runner from the left company came over to say it was set for the assault and to report the location of targets it wanted taken care of when it started ahead. I went over to Byrnes and got similar information from him. He told me he had suffered some casualties from the artillery fire and air attack but not as many as he had feared and his company still was plenty strong enough to keep going. Byrnes' company became another of those "lucky" outfits, like our battery and lucky for the same reason. It had Byrnes. We had Rick.

I hustled back to our telephone and gave Rick the target information. A couple of minutes later both the one-o-fives and the mediums began softening up the ridge for the assault, shifting from concentration to concentration in what seemed like split-second jumps. Then the doughboys started up the slope.

We expected real opposition here. When the light machine-gun and mortar fire from the top had dwindled, it had only made us suspicious. We shouldn't have been. That assault wasn't much more than a hillside stroll. When the doughboys reached the top, almost without the loss of a man, there wasn't an able-bodied Jerry anywhere around.

A couple of minutes later, Barney and I were up with Byrnes with the radio and Furman and Warren were extending the telephone line again. There was some heavy firing off to the left but, in our zone, we had taken our first objective so easily that the assault, if you can call it that, seemed like an anticlimax.

We felt pretty good about it, though, and, so far as the detail was concerned, we thought we had been forward observing to beat hell. We didn't stop patting ourselves on the back until it began to soak in that we hadn't scored the greatest victory since Gettysburg and that all we had been up against was very light rear guard action. Most of the enemy who had been on that ridge had beat it long before we arrived.

All we could see ahead of us was more hills and no Jerries. A few were around, lingering behind their pals to give with machine-gun bullets but that worked both ways. When they fired, we spotted them and that would be that. But the main enemy force opposite us was much farther back. It stayed back, never putting up a real fight. As soon as we spotted them and began to pour artillery fire on their positions, they would backtrack. It began to get monotonous. The orders were to turn their flank, but you can't do that, when the flank keeps retreating, straight back.

Rick telephoned that the fight over in the center had been a tough one for three hours, then the tanks had broken through. He said the Jerries on our side probably were retreating to keep abreast of their other units.

By noon there wasn't any doubt that the Jerries were running, so fast even the doughboys began moving up in their trucks. There were some skirmishes and the artillery had some work to do and once in a while the opposition threatened to show fight but never for long. By nightfall, we were many miles from our starting point of the morning.

All of us in the detail were tired. We hadn't had much sleep since daybreak of the day before and we had been scrambling all over our zone whenever we stopped long enough to make it look like action. And we all felt a little let down. This wasn't the kind of fight we had expected. Furman had had the toughest job of all. Our howitzers had moved forward five times during the day and, each time, Furman had had to reel in all his wire and then unreel it again.

We didn't stop with the coming of night. The enemy kept on retreating and we kept following them. We were up a couple more miles by morning, when we tried to pin them into a fight again. But it was the same story as the day before.

The Jerries slowed down considerably but they still retreated.

We didn't even pay much attention to the thing that should have worried us most—squadrons of enemy fighters and bombers which came over us high and kept right on going. Looking back, we sometimes could see them in dogfights with our planes far behind our positions and the Jerries always came off second best. But, always, a little later more of them would go over.

Major Barlow's battalion was in reserve that day so we worked with the third battalion and I didn't see Byrnes again until his company came back late that night. When we got together, we decided it was a pretty good war and all it had needed up to now was the American touch. The next second, we both admitted we weren't so sure. Rick came up for a while, not a bit optimistic. He said we were going too fast, faster than our supply lines could keep up with us, especially with enemy bombers concentrating on them. He said that was what they had been doing that afternoon and causing plenty of damage.

"The trouble is," he said, "the Jerries are falling back on their supply bases and we're running away from ours. I just wish we had more ammunition and were sure a lot more would come through in the next few hours."

Just after he left us, it began to rain—in bucketfuls. For a while it was almost a cloudburst and it kept up intermittently all night. By morning, the ground was gumbo. It didn't look good for our tanks. But it didn't seem to make much difference on our sector. It was foggy early in the morning and decent observation was almost impossible but not much seemed necessary. The doughboys kept right on splashing ahead through the mud.

Then the sun came out—nice, bright, hot African sun. It drove away the fog but it replaced that with the steam it raised from the damp ground and we steamed with it. It wasn't much fun with all the clothes we had on, including our raincoats, and all the junk we always had to carry. The only consolation was that the sun was drying the ground so fast it was becoming easier to move.

By nine o'clock we were under full headway again. The terrain was rugged here, too rugged to see very far in any direction. Hills obstructed the view on all sides. It was perfect country for defense but the Heinies still didn't seem inclined to take advantage of it. Then the firing became heavy on our left, heavier than at any time since the first morning. Rick telephoned that our center was beginning to hit stiff opposition and wasn't moving ahead as fast as we were.

Shortly before noon, it suddenly began to look as if we were going to accomplish what we had set out to do. The enemy front seemed to be bending. We definitely were pushing back their flank, turning it. By noon, we had turned it to the extent that we were headed northeast instead of due east as we had been before. And then, just after noon, we ran head on into the first real opposition we had had.

The Jerries were in a very strong position, no stronger than others they had passed up but they seemed to have decided to stand by their guns here. When the doughboys tried to advance, they ran into such a heavy storm of lead that both the left company and Byrnes' had to pull back into defilade until the artillery could pave a better road for them.

We were well ahead of our batteries but the enemy positions still were within easy range of our howitzers. When they opened up, the Jerries had seemed to have more stuff than before but I still wasn't worried. I crawled out on a rise where I could get a better view of things and began looking for definite targets.

When I called Rick, though, he told me we would have to wait. The battalion was having its hands full taking care of the left battalion of infantry which was running into trouble.

"You're far enough out anyway," he said, "you can wait until the rest catch up."

"How about turning the flank while we can?" I asked him.

"You mean *when* we can," he said. "Right now, we can't."

Byrnes had just received word from Major Barlow along the same lines. Both of us were disappointed but there was nothing we could do.

Things became very quiet in our zone. Once in a while some machine gun would pepper away at our position and one of Byrnes' men would return the compliment but that was all. There was plenty of racket on our left, which made us all the more anxious to get going again. When I called Rick again to ask when we might expect some fires, he said he didn't know and he sounded worried. He said the battalion ammunition was running lower than he liked. There was just enough to use where it would do the most good. The enemy planes were blasting at our supply lines so heavily that ammunition was coming through only in dribbles.

I don't like to talk about what happened after that. I became restless, waiting for things to happen and thought I had better spend the time doing everything I could to prepare for the time when our hows could go to work in our zone again. I spotted a crest away out in front of us which promised a swell view of the enemy positions. It was the first time I had picked an observation point far up ahead of the doughboys and I felt very daring about the whole thing. Through my binoculars I could see a couple of shell holes up there which seemed tailor-made for us.

Since we had plenty of time, we went up the safe way, circling around through defilades which screened us completely and we went up one at a time. One of the shell holes was perfect for observation without being too exposed. Behind it and down the crest a few yards was an equally good spot where Barney dug in his radio. When Furman brought the telephone in, I told him to find himself a place near

Barney and take a rest and I sent Warren back to Byrnes to keep in touch there so he could signal me if anything came up. Then I stretched out in the shell hole, shaded my binoculars so no light would reflect from the glass and began observing.

I just lay there and observed all over the place, spotting targets and charting them on my map, patting myself on the back, thinking how good I was and how brave to be away out there, the most advanced American soldier on the front. Oh, sure, I conceded that Barney and Furman who were down there just behind me, were very brave, too.

Every fifteen minutes, I called Rick and told him how peaceful it was in our little world. Nothing bothered me. Nothing disturbing crossed my mind, not even the shortage of ammunition. That would come through all right. Nothing could stop us. As soon as the left battalion proved it was as good as the gang we were with, it would be a breeze and we could start for the Mediterranean again.

Another fifteen minutes passed and I called Rick again, reported and asked how the boys on the left were doing in all the racket they were making.

"Not so good," he said, "it looks as if they have hit us with strong reinforcements. You're sure everything is all right where you are?"

"Couldn't be all righter," I said brightly.

Byrnes crawled up to my shell hole, looking worried. "I don't like it," he said. "They're too quiet over there."

I said I thought they were just lying low, waiting for us to stick our necks out.

"I wonder," he said and his face was full of trouble, "I don't like it. I've sent some men out trying to learn what goes on."

He went back to his company and I went on observing, although I had covered just about everything in sight. The firing on our left seemed to be getting heavier. I say "seemed" because when there's a lot of firing, especially in rough country like that, it's easy to mistake just where the shell bursts are sounding off. But, if I had been on my toes, instead of feeling so contented with myself, I might have begun to use my head and I might have doped things a little more accurately.

Anyway, there was an exceptional amount of firing going on and I just took it for granted it was all on our left when I called Rick again.

I heard an odd, crackling sound behind him when he came in but I paid no attention to it. I said, "Everything quiet on the northeastern front." And then he let me have it.

"Quiet!" he yelled. "Quiet! You damned idiot! Get back here quick or you'll be quiet in a concentration camp."

"What the hell?" I said, a little sore.

"The Jerries are on us with tanks," Rick came back. "We're fighting with our carbines!" Then the line went dead.

# VIII

WHEN I HUNG UP, a little dizzy, what I thought of myself as a forward observer couldn't have been repeated in a smoking room. I was still groggy when I saw Warren heading for the shell hole as fast as he could crawl, making wild signals every few seconds.

About that time I came to and my ears began to work. For the first time I realized a lot of the firing was directly behind us and when I looked through my binoculars, the battle smoke was plainly visible, rising from our battalion position behind the intervening hills. Over the edge of the shell hole, I yelled down to Barney to pack up as we were getting out of there fast. He came to life faster than I had and he had his cases packed, separated and ready before I reached him. I could see Byrnes signaling frantically in my direction, waving toward the rear. His men already were crawling back.

Those were good boys in the detail. When Warren came up, he automatically grabbed for one of the radio cases. Furman scrambled into the shell hole, disconnected the telephone instrument and started to reel up the wire. There wasn't time for that, of course. I told him to forget it and relay with the others in carrying the radio set. "And drop that, if you have to," I said, because the Heinies across the way were showing signs of life and they might head our way any minute. Three carbines and an automatic didn't seem quite enough fire power to hold them off. We went away from there as fast as we could crawl, just in time to miss the enemy fire which began spraying around our shell hole. We tried going even faster when Jack gave us his news.

He said Major Barlow had telephoned Lieutenant Byrnes

while he was there. The dope was that Jerry reinforcements from Von Arnim had sneaked up during the rain and fog and hid out behind the hills away off to our right, outside the battle line. Then they just waited until the Jerries we were chasing had pulled us around where they wanted us. When the ground was dry enough for the tanks to move they had come out and headed straight for our artillery. Major Barlow said our left battalion was being pushed back and the other Jerries had moved in so fast on our flank that we had a swell chance of being surrounded before we could get back. It certainly sounded as if the firing were coming from all sides.

All four of us took turns on the radio cases, but they slowed us down for the first couple of hundred yards while we were hustling down the slope. When we were just about out of sight from the enemy positions behind us, we decided it was just as safe to be on our feet and make a run for it as to creep along so slowly anyone could overhaul us.

We finally caught up with Byrnes who was directing the rear guard of course. He was as sore at himself as I was at me and we made the air blue, expressing ourselves as we went along. He was bothered most by the fact that he hadn't received any warning from the men he had stationed far enough over to have seen what was coming. We found out about that later. Every one of the outposts had been picked off by the Nazis for whom our respect had sunk so low a couple of hours before.

They taught us a lot that day and one of the lessons was that outposts can not be sent out singly in this war. They must go in pairs to keep a lookout in all directions at once. When they go alone, they just disappear. The marines already had learned that on Guadalcanal but we hadn't heard about it.

With almost every step we took, the firing seemed to be heavier ahead of us and it was spreading beyond the battery positions. The implications of that made us feel worse than ever.

We were in such a hurry, we almost forgot we had a jeep parked back here until we practically stumbled over it. We didn't know how good an idea it was to drive it into a battle but we didn't care much and it certainly offered the quickest means of getting where we wanted to go, so Warren jumped in and started the motor.

Furman looked in the back and said, sort of mournfully, "I've lost so much wire there's even room for me." For some reason, it struck us as funny and we roared. You laugh at curious things at a time like that. But it broke the tension and we all felt better.

We didn't want to leave Byrnes but we had no choice. Our job was to return to the battery as fast as we could make it —if there still was a battery. We didn't know what to expect by now. But, while we were piling into the jeep, a runner came up to Byrnes and told him an enemy infantry outfit was cutting in toward us and the only possible way back was by a sharp oblique movement which would carry us well beyond the old battery position.

Right there, Byrnes stopped rear guarding. He asked us to take him up ahead in a hurry and crowded into the jeep, hanging on by his teeth. We plowed along behind the hills until we reached the spot where Byrnes' riflemen were firing from the crest. Warren was all for driving straight to the top so we could get in a couple of personal shots but I told him to keep the jeep where it was while Byrnes and I did a little scouting.

What we saw from the hill wasn't encouraging. The enemy tanks had had difficult going in the half-dried ground and quite a number of them seemed to be wrecked but the rest were still moving forward. Their infantry was swarming up on foot, some of them among the tanks. One company had deployed toward us. Our battery was gone and the fight was well past where it had been. We only hoped it had been able to get away all right. Some of our own tanks were coming into the fight and we could see some doughboys giving the Jerries some opposition with machine guns and anti-tank guns but not enough to stop them. It looked bad.

Byrnes barked a couple of orders and his men began deploying along the hills, pumping away with their rifles and machine guns. He spread his men out to cover as much front as possible then began rolling them in from the left so his line of fire kept edging toward our troops. He had at least 75 per cent of his men constantly firing and, at the same time was making his oblique retreat. If he got away with it, he finally would connect up with our other forces without ever having stopped his holding action. He was enfilading the enemy with fire they hadn't expected even while he was saving his company.

We shook hands and wished each other luck and then our jeep was on its way as fast as it could take the terrain, keeping below the crest of the hills so we wouldn't be exposed any sooner than necessary. We circled wide when we finally were opposite the fight itself and all of us took a couple of deep breaths as we shot out from behind the hills and started across the open.

Warren took the jeep through like a broken field runner, zigzagging like the end of a four weeks' jag. Looking back I could see Byrnes still coming and doing such a good job, it seemed as if he would make it.

We began to hear machine-gun bullets whistling past and then heavy shells began splattering around us, some of them too darned close.

"They can't mean us," Barney said. "That's too much ammunition to waste on a jeep."

"Not if I'm in it," Furman said. Barney laughed and Furman's face went red and, over the noise, he yelled, "I mean—I don't mean—I mean—" and then he gave up.

The shellfire was getting so heavy, it seemed best to abandon the jeep but Warren raised a howl. He begged me to let him take it through, even if the rest of us got out. Then Barney and Furman yelled they wanted to stay with it, too. Maybe it wasn't being a good officer but it seemed as if our chances of getting through were about as good in the jeep as on our stomachs so I told Jack to go ahead. We'd all stick.

That decision paid off a lot of times, later. It did something to us and for us which we never lost, sticking together and staying with our equipment the first time we were in a jam.

Then we were running through a lot of doughboys who were heading into the fight. We stopped an officer and asked him if he knew anything about the one-o-fives. He waved toward some hills on our left and said he believed what was left of them was there. While we looked, there were several puffs of smoke from the hills and then we heard the crack that comes only from a one-o-five howitzer. The trouble was, there weren't enough of them.

Warren yelled, "The home stretch!" and stepped on the gas, heading straight for the hills, just as another shower of shells dropped around us. Warren yelled, "Ouch!" and the jeep swerved for a second but he straightened it out again. I could see his face had gone white and asked him if he had been hit. He said his arm had been nicked but he could make it all right. It was no time to stop for first aid but when I leaned over to look, there already was a lot of blood on his left sleeve and the sleeve itself was badly torn.

Then another shell hit and I felt as if somebody had struck me over the head with a baseball bat. My helmet seemed to have gone with the wind. After the first jolt, I felt a stinging sensation above my right temple and blood was running down my face so I knew I'd been hit but not seriously.

Barney yelled, "Hey!" and whipped out the first aid kit. He crouched forward and began wrapping gauze around my head. I told him he'd better do something about Warren but Jack said he was okay, he needed both hands to drive and could be fixed up later.

The small number of one-o-fives in action had us all on edge when we finally bounced up the reverse slope of the elevation from which they were shooting. The situation there wasn't so good and we saw no sign of the Battery C howitzers or gun crews. I spotted the battalion commander, hopped out of the jeep and hurried over to him. When I asked him about Battery C, his face went sober and he told me it was back of the next hill. I asked him where the battery's howitzers were. He looked queer and said, "There aren't any—not any more."

"Captain Hallon?" I asked.

"He's with his men," the CO said. "You had better report to him."

So we bounced back as fast as we could go, swung around the hill and there, in a deep ravine, was Battery C—what was left of it. It didn't look as if more than half the men were there and the only officers in sight were Rick and Bob Dolan.

As we drove up, it sounded as if the battle were coming closer and the firing were heavier. A mass of enemy planes had come in, dropping bombs and machine-gunning our troops but now our own fliers were diving into the mess. More of our tanks were swinging toward the flank but it sounded as if we still were being pushed back. We were hardly conscious of this, though, when we climbed out of the jeep and looked at the battery. We only felt sick. I told Furman and Barney to fix up Warren's arm and I headed for Rick.

He looked at me as if I were a ghost but the first thing he said was, "Where's your helmet?" and then, "Here, take this one," and he picked up one lying near his feet and handed it to me. Then he said, "What happened to you?"

"Nothing," I said, "we all made it. Where's the medical officer? Warren needs him."

He told me and I yelled at Furman to take over the jeep and drive Jack back for repairs. Rick called out, "Hold it, here's another passenger," and started pushing me toward the car.

I said, "I'm all right. It's just a nick. Tell me what happened to the battery."

"We were on the outside," Rick said. "It was up to us. We just had time to turn our hows when the tanks came. We got as many as we could but they ran over us. Our hows weren't captured. They were smashed—every one of them. And every one of them kept on firing until it was smashed. We couldn't pull out. We were the only defense line there was until the doughboy reserves came in.

"We slowed them down a little but we didn't have enough to stop them. It was point-blank fire. We couldn't miss. Neither could they. Two of Battery B's guns stayed and went the same way. That let Battery A and the other half of B get away. When our hows went, we didn't have anything left to fight with except our carbines and the four machine guns and we lost two of those. Barrett was wounded the first ten minutes, we haven't heard yet how badly. What were left of us finally got back here. Look at 'em, Jim. My God, look at 'em." He was almost in tears. Then he looked at me and said, "Go and get your head fixed up."

I told him I'd rather stay, that I wanted to do something, anything that would help. I said, "I feel it's mostly my fault."

For the first time, Rick looked as if he were sore. "Don't talk like a damned fool," he said. "Now get out of here. That's an order."

I went over to the jeep, my feet dragging. I had never felt so low in my life.

"None of us were feeling very high when we took the lieutenant and Jack to the field dressing station," Barney Johns interpolated, "Furman and I didn't know whether they'd be shipped back. Everybody at the station was working like mad because, the way the fight was going, nobody knew how soon the whole shebang might have to pack up and run. So you can imagine how we felt when, after about half an hour, both of them came out, all fancy with new bandages, and climbed back into the jeep."

They were glad enough to get rid of us (Kennard continued), they had so many serious cases which had to go to the base hospital. Warren had lost a lot of blood and they wanted to keep him in bed for a couple of days but he said there was nothing wrong with him a couple of meals and some sleep wouldn't fix so they let him go.

Personally, I wasn't feeling as cheerful as the other fellows while we were on our way back to the battery. I had a stiff headache, not from the cut in my forehead but from the realization of how I had muffed my first FO job. If I had used my head, I wouldn't have picked that shell hole for observation which made me feel so brave. It was away up on the left of our zone when I should have picked a spot as far to the right as I could go where I could keep a weather eye open to make sure the Nazis didn't try the same flank turning stunt on us that we were using on them. Maybe I couldn't have seen them in that maze of hills. Both Rick and Byrnes said later the chances were a thousand to one I couldn't have. The trouble is, I'll never know and, anyway, I should have been over there. It was part of my job to watch for enemy movements in other places than just my zone of observation.

I figured it was a simple cinch I'd never have another chance at forward observing and that I'd probably find myself in Casablanca, checking bills of lading, or maybe be shipped back to the United States. I couldn't see that I deserved anything else.

What happened to me didn't seem very important, though, when we reported back at the battery. Everybody knew it had done a terrific job that afternoon but Rick was heartsick, not about the guns, and other matériel but about the men he had lost. Rick was a strict disciplinarian but he looked upon every man in the battery as his personal friend and treated him that way. When we came up, he had finished his checkup and his voice shook when he told us—seventeen men killed and twenty-seven wounded, most of them seriously—nearly half the battery's strength. Only seven men from those crack gun crews came out unwounded. Rick's own escape had been close to miraculous. He took over the howitzers when Barrett was wounded and stayed with them to the finish. The concussion from the shell which smashed our last one had knocked him flat and he was practically out when Schwartz, the only man left from that last gun crew, had dragged him back and put him in a truck—the last battery truck to get away.

Rick and I had chow together but we didn't talk much. When I tried to tell him how I felt about my own performance he told me again to stop talking like a fool. He said we all were to blame and that maybe we'd be a little smarter next time.

Of course, there wasn't anything we could do except pull back to some place where we could reorganize. The reserves which had been tossed into the fight slowed the Jerries down and, since they don't like to fight at night much, things quieted down a good deal after dark. But Rick said we didn't have enough stuff to stop the force we were up against now and that there would be more retreating.

A battalion of lights which had come a lot of miles in a hurry moved in to relieve us fairly early in the evening and we packed up and started back. I kept trying to learn if Byrnes had come through all right and, just before we left, had word he was okay and, in view of the fight it had put up, his company had suffered surprisingly few casualties. But the whole infantry regiment had been mauled as badly as our battalion so it was pulling out, too.

Warren was fit for duty by the time we reached our base and I hadn't needed more than an adhesive patch after the first twenty-four hours so the detail was still intact. We had word, too, that Barrett was not seriously wounded and would be back in two or three weeks. The other news we heard was that, behind us, the Jerries had been stopped after pushing our troops back for two days.

In the rear area bivouac, we were issued new howitzers and other equipment and all the battery casualties were replaced. Rick corralled some good men, all fully trained, of course, so, in a few days, we knew the battery would be okay again. But there wasn't much time to whip them into shape. Intermittent showers interfered during the few days we did have and then came the orders for us to move up again.

The front already took in a good deal more territory than when we had left it with more and more British and Americans going in every day, and the rumor was out that our forces were getting set for one more stab to reach Tunis and Bizerte before the rains bogged us down completely.

*

# IX

WHEN WE REACHED the front again, it didn't take us long to learn we had left the kindergarten and now were in at least a grade school war. We had been sent in to strengthen a spot where the Americans were trying to shoulder their way into a better position for the hopoff when the real drive started and the Jerries weren't giving us any real estate free.

When Rick and I went up for reconnaissance late in the afternoon before we moved in, the doughboys were consolidating a position they had just taken and were beating off attempts to recapture it. We spent a good deal of the time on our faces while enemy fire splashed around, getting the lay of the land and whatever other information we could between shell bursts. We stayed long enough to make sure that part of the country would still be in our hands when the doughboys of our own combat team came up and infantry action had practically stopped when we went back.

The artillery on both flanks of our zone gave us heavy protective fire when we came up after dark but plenty came our way, giving us our first experience in taking up a new position under fire. It wasn't too easy. That was the night we decided to go in for foxholes instead of slit trenches. They felt healthier. Of the detail, Furman had the toughest time. Shellfire broke the telephone lines twice even before he could run them all the way to our observation post and check them through. There wasn't any doubt about it. The Jerries didn't like our holding that ground.

The best thing about the situation was that we were working with Byrnes again. We both felt we had personal scores to settle and hoped to make the first payment in the morning when his company was going to spearhead a try for the next ridge.

It didn't work out quite that way. Shortly before daylight, one of Byrnes' patrols came in and reported hearing tanks assembling and then, fifteen minutes before we were scheduled to start firing our mapped concentrations, the enemy artillery opened up on us with the heaviest fire we had been under so far. I had reported to Rick and the fire direction center, of course, and had been told both the one-o-fives and mediums were standing by to work on the tanks if they attacked.

At the same time, the doughboys moved up their heavy weapons—antitank guns, mortars and cannon—through the shellfire and took advanced positions. It was still too dark to see much of what was going on across the way so when the enemy fire suddenly stepped up, Byrnes sent some flare rockets over no man's land and that wiped out all doubt. Tanks —lots of them—were rolling out from their positions and headed in our direction.

The number of them gave us a jolt. This was going to take a different kind of forward observing from any we had done before. Under the flares, Warren and I made a quick guess as to the range and I telephoned it in. The battery salvo was too far over the leading tanks. We pulled down the range enough to allow for the progress of the tanks and called for fire for effect and all our one-o-fives and mediums opened up.

The glare of the bursts showed we were on the tanks. One of them started to burn and, through our binoculars, we could see a couple of men flop out of the turret. The rest kept coming, all of them zigzagging now.

It was getting lighter every second so adjusting fire was easier but it still was tough enough, especially as it was our first whirl at this kind of job. We could see the tanks spread out all the way back to the ridge so we kept our fire where it was until the leading tanks were well out in front of it, then pulled down the range again. Two more tanks were hit and started to burn but this wasn't even a dent in that fleet.

Then everything seemed to happen at once. It was full daylight now and we had pulled the range down twice more but the tanks were still coming and those out front began firing. The doughboys suddenly opened up with all their heavy weapons. The enemy artillery kept pounding at us. Through our glasses we could see their infantry pouring out of their foxholes to follow up the tanks. Some time in the middle of things, squadrons of swastika planes came over and swooped down on our positions, bombing and machine-gunning. They knocked out two of the doughboy cannon and some of the antitank guns but the rest kept pumping away. Then a flock of our own planes came boiling out of the sky and a mass dogfight started upstairs. And always the tanks kept coming. Rick cut in to tell me the Long Toms—our heavies—were coming in and while we shortened the range some more, our fire became heavier and still we weren't getting enough of the tanks. A plane came streaking down in flames, then another. We kept on reducing the range. The leading tanks were only a thousand yards away, then nine hundred, eight hundred, seven hundred. Another plane crashed, over on the far side of no man's land where the enemy infantry was moving up. We could see them scattering away from the burning plane. We pulled down our range again and our shells were pouring in so thick and fast it didn't seem possible any of the tanks could get through but they did. Rick cut in again to say all the artillery within range was coming in. They did, just as we called for fire on a line only three hundred yards in front of us. This had to do it. We didn't dare drop our shells any closer to our own positions. The concentration was terrific. The whole area in front of us was just one merry, blazing hell while we held our breath. Two tanks came zigzagging through it, then another, then one more—and that was all. Through the smoke, we could see all the rest of them turn tail and head for home. We finally had stopped them.

The four which did get through never had a chance. The pair in front were within two hundred yards of us before they seemed to realize the jig was up. When they tried to turn back it was too late. The doughboys gave them everything they had and the tanks exploded right in our faces. One of the other two wavered and stopped. Its turret hatch opened and the crew piled out and came our way, hands in the air. The fourth tank was broadside on when it was hit by half a dozen projectiles and it just collapsed in a burning heap. Nobody came out of it alive.

So now the fire direction was all in reverse. It was up the range and up it again to catch as many of the tanks as we could before they reached port. The enemy infantry already was backtracking.

Byrnes came over and flopped beside the foxhole. All he said was, "Phew!" and I was ready to double that. We took out cigarettes and tried to light them and then we both laughed. Our hands were shaking so much we could hardly make it.

As our artillery fire rolled farther and farther from us across no man's land, we could see wrecked and burning tanks all over the place. Almost a third of the armor which had attacked us had been knocked out. The air fight was over, too, with our planes chasing what was left of the swastikas.

But there was no letup for us. Before the last tank was out of sight, the orders came through to go ahead with our original plan and hit the Jerries while they still were groggy from the licking they had just taken. Byrnes hustled over to his company and almost as soon as we had begun firing the charted concentrations, the doughboys were on their way. By the time we had finished those, they were so far ahead we had to pick up and follow them. The terrain was a mess, torn up by shellfire and dotted with wrecked tanks, dead

Jerries and some of the planes which had been shot down, and it took us quite a while to catch up with Byrnes.

Then we still kept going. It was a walk through. Apparently the enemy had abandoned the ridge as soon as they saw the doughboys coming and had pulled back far enough to give themselves a chance to catch their breath and reorganize. They did a good job of it. After we had taken the ridge practically without casualties, we ran into nothing but trouble. We tried to push on because the position we really wanted was still ahead but the Jerries stood their ground and began slugging it out.

All that day and the next we just inched ahead, grabbing a rise here and another one there but not actually getting anywhere. We had trouble with communications all the time. During the first afternoon, Furman had to fix the lines seven times under fire. At one time when the wire was out, the radio was damaged by a spent shell splinter and Barney had to do an emergency repair job, also under fire. Warren literally had his binoculars shot out of his hands. A slug which just missed his fingers hit the glasses and broke them into smithereens. Most of the time the going was so thick and spotting targets was so difficult he and I divided the zone of observation with each of us taking over half to be sure of covering it all.

By the end of the second day, Byrnes' company, which had been carrying the load, was worn down to a nubbin and had to be relieved. The company which took over was commanded by a man we didn't know, a Captain Sommers, up front for the first time.

By this time the infantry and artillery weren't throwing rocks at each other any more. In the first battle, the doughboys found out how valuable the artillery can be to them and after that, they were pretty much for us. We still weren't exactly palsy walsy but the only doughboys who still looked at us out of the corners of their eyes were those who hadn't been through the mill. Sommers was one of these, suspicious of everything the artillery did, especially the FO detail. But he was a good infantryman and smart enough to give us all the co-operation he could. For value received, of course.

We converted him, though. Orders came through for an attack at four o'clock in the morning which we hoped would turn out to be a surprise. For his part of the punch, Sommers needed some especially well-timed and accurate artillery fire. When we gave it to him and made the going easy, he seemed almost as surprised as the Heinies, who thought the whole thing was unfair, and he began to thaw out. Naturally, the detail had to go along as there was no other way of keeping contact with him in the dark. That surprised him, too, and he thawed out some more. A little later, when the Jerries were awake and fighting back, his company was stopped cold by a heavy machine-gun concentration. Barney set up his radio in a shell hole and we had the battalion dropping shells on the MGs while Sommers was still on his way over to ask us if we could do anything about it. That clinched it.

He looked over where the one-o-five shells were dropping dead on the target, then turned to me, cleared his throat and said, "Nice work." Then we both started to laugh and when I soft-soaped it a little by saying the artillery had to be on its toes for doughboys who could step out like his, we were practically buddies. It wasn't long before I thought he was second only to Byrnes.

By daylight, we were a lot nearer our main objective than we had been the night before but then the Jerries collected themselves and began slugging back again, taking advantage of every possible defense position to hold us off as long as possible. Twice they tried to counterattack but we managed to get the range on them and the combination of our artillery and the infantry heavy weapons and machine guns stopped them although once the whole detail had to do a

fast back scramble to keep out of their way. The best observation post we could get that day was a shell hole. There just
wasn't time for digging.

That was the day we awoke to the value of working with
the infantry mortar observers. There were more targets than
the one-o-fives could handle effectively. A good many of them
were the spot kind which is mortar meat. The mortars were
handling them, too. The trouble was, we didn't have close
enough contact with the mortars to know which targets they
would take on.

So we tried working alongside their observers whenever
we could and keeping in touch with them all the time so we
could decide in advance whether mortars or hows should
handle targets about which there was any question. It worked
from the start and that made another lesson learned.

Early in the afternoon, it began to cloud up, heavy and
dark. By that time, with every outfit edging its way ahead
wherever and whenever it could, there wasn't anything re-
sembling a front line. Our leading elements were zigzagged
all over the place. Once, when I was talking to Rick on the
telephone, he told me Sommers' company was making faster
progress than any other outfit, and it wouldn't be long before
the hows would have to move up. By sixteen hundred, we
knew we were at the point of a salient, closer to the enemy
than we had been at any time. Opposite us here they weren't
more than four or five hundred yards away.

The sky was completely overcast now and Sommers wanted
to push the Jerries out of their position before it rained. We
caught up with him just as his company was starting forward
again. We ran into a storm of lead. To go ahead would have
been suicide so Sommers ordered his men to take cover and
dig in.

It was so murky now that observation wasn't easy but I
wanted to spot the machine guns and mortars which had
stopped us and I edged over to the left for a better view.

Barney and Warren set up the radio in a shell hole and I crawled into another one farther up with the remote control. Before I had any reason to use it, though, Furman came up with the telephone. After he had checked the line, he eased himself into another shell hole. There were a lot of them around there.

A foggy haze was spreading over everything and I was about ready to give up hope of seeing anything when the boys across the way decided to help me by spraying Sommers' position with their machine guns and mortars again. From the tip-off given by the sound of them, I figured their position as best I could and called the fire direction center but Rick answered the telephone. He said the other batteries were moving up and Battery C was handling the cover fires. I gave him the fire mission and the adjusting round came over just as it began to rain.

# X

In a couple of seconds the rain was coming down in sheets. It was so blinding I couldn't see anything fifty yards away. I told Rick to fire for effect but I couldn't tell from where I was when and if the mission was accomplished so I was going to edge up for a closer look.

I took the remote control with me and worked my way forward about a hundred yards, not worrying about being careful because the enemy couldn't see any better than I could in that cloudburst. I found a shell hole half full of water but I already was soaked and crouching in a little water couldn't make me any damper so I slid into it. I still couldn't see much. The firing was subsiding all along the front. Opposite us, the Jerries had become absolutely quiet but Battery C still was pumping shells into their positions.

Then I had the jolt of my life. Straight ahead of me, a half dozen Jerries suddenly loomed out of the rain. Then I made out a lot more of them and it struck me this was no rainstorm patrol but a counterattack. I ducked my head below the edge of the shell hole, so I was practically up to my neck in water, and, in about ten seconds, called Barney and told him to get word to Sommers quick.

Then I scrambled out of the shell hole and started slogging back toward the detail. It didn't seem like a good day to play Horatio at the bridge. I thought I was going to get away with it when I heard that rat-tat-tat and bullets whizzing by me. I ducked behind a rock, pulled out my automatic and emptied it at them. I hit a grand total of one and I think I only winged him. But the Jerries flopped on their faces and stopped for a few seconds, which helped.

I pushed a spare clip into my gun and headed for home again. I was lucky for a minute because the Jerries didn't know it was just the Lone Ranger out there and they were still down. I gained another ten or fifteen yards before they came to. Just as I dodged behind another rock, a couple of them yelled, *"Offizier!"* and why not? I had the tag on me— a pistol belt and no weapon but an automatic. They let fly but I was behind a good-sized boulder and kept on being lucky. Peeking around the rock, I saw them start a rush for me and I emptied my lovely automatic once more. My average held. I winged another one and the rest slowed up just long enough for me to slip away from the rock and roll part way down hill out of sight. Then I crawled up to the shell hole where I had left Barney with the radio set.

I tumbled into it and had another shock when I saw Barney was firing his carbine toward the left at some Heinies who had no business coming from that direction at all. Warren was in another shell hole about ten feet away, firing at the gang which had surprised me. Then Furman, who had taken the message to Sommers, flopped into our shell hole, yanked his carbine off his shoulders and started to fire back in the direction of our battery position. I thought he was crazy until I made out some dim figures crawling up from his side. We were practically surrounded.

While I was reloading my clips, Furman said Captain Sommers wanted us to get to him. I said it was a little late for that, because as soon as we stopped firing and tried to get away, the Heinies would rush us and grab us before we were half way to the company.

Barney looked at me over his shoulder and grinned. "So we play Custer," he said.

He wasn't far wrong. The Heinies started a rush at us from three sides. The reason they had us from three directions, of course, was because of the raggedness of the front,. which made it easy for any fairly small group to sneak behind the lines of the opposition, particularly us, as we were well ahead of the troops on our left. In that downpour it was especially simple to slip through any gap in the front.

Just as the Heinies started for our shell hole, we heard Sommers' doughboys start shooting their rifles and machine guns and there were louder bursts which sounded like grenades and that meant action at close quarters. It also meant we four were distinctly on our own.

We didn't have time to think about that, though. About all that flashed through our minds was that this was it for everybody in the detail. The doughboys were more than seventy-five yards away and it was a certainty some of the enemy would move into that gap so we would be entirely surrounded. The only thing in our favor was the rain which was coming down heavier than ever so the Heinies couldn't see how few of us there were.

When they came at us, the advantage was with us for a couple of seconds because we knew exactly where they were and three carbines in good hands can do a lot of damage while my automatic at least made noise. This was the first time we had been at close grips with the enemy and the first time the fellows ever had had occasion to use their carbines but they went at it like veterans. They weren't just shooting off their guns. They were hitting live targets, firing carefully and deliberately but fast enough so it must have seemed as if a dozen rifles were in that shell hole. Anyway, enough of the Heinies dropped so that the rest stopped and pulled back.

While they were hesitating, Warren crawled over to us and said, "There's another shell hole—a big one—about ten yards over. I think we can make it. They'll start pouring it in here in a minute and we might as well let them shoot where we ain't." Barney didn't want to go. He almost bawled when he said, "How about my radio?" Warren said, "Papa will buy you a new one if you're a good boy."

We learned how smart Jack was in a very few moments.

We had crawled about two thirds of the way to the other shell hole when the Jerries came out of the blinding rain in another three-way rush, firing everything they had at the radio hole. It gave us time to fall into the new shell hole and square away to start shooting again. I don't know if I hit anybody with my automatic but not many of the carbine shots were wasted. We didn't expect to get away but we were making it very expensive for the other side.

Odd things stay in your memory of situations like that. What I remember most clearly was Barney's private war. He was on the side facing the shell hole we had left and he was firing away, muttering under his breath, "Keep away from that radio, you stinking so-and-so" and then he'd send another bullet at some Jerry who was just reaching the radio.

Then the expected happened. Some of the enemy started coming at us from the doughboy side and now we had to fire in four directions. Of course, by now, the others knew we had moved and turned their guns on us. Then Furman yelled, "Damn!" and began trying to fire his carbine with just his right hand. His left shoulder was bleeding. I slipped a new clip into my automatic and handed it to him while I took his carbine away. His face was drawn and his teeth were clenched tight from the pain but he kept on firing.

It probably was because we were making it so hot for them that the Heinies didn't move in and mop us up. We had hit at least a dozen of them and they were staying back far enough so their aim wasn't so good. Besides, it seemed to have struck them they would knock off their pals across the way if they fired too high since we were surrounded, so they were firing low and most of their lead hit the mud around the edge of the shell hole.

Still there didn't seem to be any hope. They were inching toward us and our ammunition was running low. Then it seemed to dawn upon all of us at once that the fire of the doughboys was coming nearer. At first, we thought it was a trick of our ears. Then we saw the spurts of flame from their rifles and machine guns. Some of the Jerries we knew we hadn't hit suddenly rolled over and lost interest in the fight.

The next thing we knew, a couple of squads of doughboys had fought their way through the enemy on that side and then had reached us and were cutting loose on the rest. After that, it didn't last long. The Jerries decided the surprise party was over and faded back through the rain as fast as they could scramble.

Barney was the first man out of the shell hole. For once, he forgot to be careful and ran all the way to his radio. I started to crawl out, too, and wondered why my left leg felt so stiff and numb and then Warren yelled, "Hold it, lieutenant," and pointed at my leg which was oozing blood. Then I saw that Furman had slumped down in a dead faint and I told Warren to take care of him.

One of the doughboys jumped down into the hole, ripped away my pants' leg and, for the first time, I realized a Jerry bullet had torn a gash in the fleshy part of my thigh. The doughboy made a tourniquet and stopped the bleeding, then bandaged me as best he could in that downpour. Warren said it looked as if Furman's collar-bone had been broken by the bullet which hit him, and he had kept on firing and hadn't passed out until the fight was over.

Sommers came over to say we had saved his bacon as an attack in the rain was the last thing he had expected and the warning had just given him time to get set. He was a little grim about the situation, though. He said there still were a lot of the enemy behind us and we were in a pocket but he expected to hold out until help came. He had been able to contact Major Barlow and a pretty respectable force was on its way. That meant, of course, that the wounded, including Furman and myself, couldn't get back until the reinforcements reached us.

About that time, Barney came over, carrying the remote

control which he had dragged in from where I had dropped it. He was beaming. "The set got a little shot up," he said, "but I've got it working." When he scrambled back to the radio, I called Rick and explained the situation. He said he would send up Dolan to relieve me but Warren and Barney would have to handle the telephone for a couple of days until he could get another wire man.

It was just a few minutes after that that we heard a lot of firing behind us. It kept getting heavier and nearer to us, so we knew it was our reinforcements clashing with the Jerries who had cut us off. Then the firing moved over to the left, began to sputter out, then died altogether and then our doughboys began streaming up with the word that the enemy was on the run. Dolan came up with them and another man to guide us back to the new battery position.

The rain never let up for a minute. I found I could hobble around a little but it was going to be too easy to slip on that mud in the dark so both Furman and I went back on stretchers. He went on to the base hospital, of course, but I stopped at the field dressing station. After giving me the works, the doctor said I would not have to be evacuated if I didn't try any walking for a few days. He sent me to bed and I guess I slept for about fourteen hours. When I awoke, it was still raining and I just stayed where I was. A couple of days later I could walk well enough to go back to the battery. Rick kept me there for another day or two and I served as executive officer until Barrett came back from the hospital, fit for duty. Then I went back to the detail and took Don Wills, one of the battery's regular telephone men, with me to replace Furman.

We finally had pushed the Jerries out of the positions we wanted and they had pulled back, leaving a no man's land about three thousand yards wide but, aside from that, the situation hadn't changed much. With the rainy season obviously here, it didn't look as if there would be much change for some time to come. There wasn't. Whatever drive had been planned was called off on account of wet grounds. The weather had beaten us to the punch.

Realizing that made the rainy season all the drearier, and it was dreary enough on its own account. It would rain pitchforks for two or three days and leave us swimming in mud. Then the sun would come out, bright and hot. After it had raised steam for a while, the ground would harden gradually and then, just when it was almost dry enough for action, we'd have another downpour. Of course, the FO detail kept right on working. We had to go on prowling around, keeping an eye on the enemy and looking for something to shoot at, even when the rest of the troops were immobilized.

At that, we had the best of it, because we were doing something. For most of the others, there wasn't anything except the occasional artillery fire and skirmishes between patrols. The rest of the time, it was just waiting for the wet weather to end. It got on everyone's nerves and had a good deal to do with our army's worst trouble during that rainy season—lack of discipline.

The American trait which rebels against unquestioning obedience to any kind of order is one of the things that make our soldiers such dangerous fighters because they use their heads in a pinch instead of depending upon the head man to do all the thinking. But it has its drawbacks in an army at the front and we hadn't found any happy medium as yet between "rugged individualism" and complete submission to regimentation.

Too many of our soldiers became careless—about protecting themselves, about exposing positions, about bunching in the open so they revealed troop concentrations, about parking themselves along sky lines where their silhouettes made them perfect targets. Too many still were trying to get by with slit trenches because they were less trouble to dig than foxholes. Too many of them became tired of the hot, heavy helmets and took them off in violation of orders at the same time they were being careless in the way they moved around. Too many of them became unnecessary head-wound casualties because, even if general action was stymied, both sides kept right on watching for anything or anybody that looked like a target and shooting at those they saw.

We didn't know it, but, in those days, we still were a heluva distance from being a real army. The men were wildcats in a fight but we had a tough time learning that this war isn't going to be won by soloists but by having all the cogs working together. Our gears were becoming unmeshed too often.

In all fairness to our detail, it wasn't subject to that criticism. It operated as smoothly as clockwork and the fellows saw to it themselves that none of them became careless. Wills worked into it exceptionally well. To Jack and Barney, he intimated that he considered it practically a promotion to be sent to the detail and, from then on, he was a full member of the club.

I had been a little optimistic about my leg. Between the rains and the amount of hopping around we had to do while we were on the job, it did not heal as quickly as I had hoped and the reliefs we had were mighty welcome. At that time, after every three-day stretch up front, we would have a day off with Dolan taking over with a couple of radio and telephone men from the battery who made up a sort of secondary detail.

It was about the middle of January that I slipped in the mud and practically knocked myself out. The leg stiffened and Rick ordered me to rest a few days at the battery position. After four days of it, when my leg was just beginning to unlimber again, Rick told me he had been called to Algiers for a couple of days and I might as well go along as I was useless around the battery anyway. The doctor okayed the trip. He said it probably would do me more good than staying in the mud. Rick didn't tell me what his mission was and I didn't ask him. It was none of my business. I was satisfied just to go along.

A jeep took us back to the airfield where a plane was waiting for us. Less than two hours later, we were in Algiers.

# XI

WE LOOKED LIKE HELL. They forgot to include laundry and pants pressing service in the army tables of organization and equipment for war in Tunisia. But when we reached the hotel room which had been staked out for us, we found the American influence had instituted a fast service for field stained uniforms like ours, so we had a chance to clean up before Rick had to report at headquarters.

While we waited for our clothes, we took turns wallowing in the first hot bath we'd had since landing in Africa. Then, to our surprise, our uniforms did come back, all bright and shining, sooner than we had expected. Since we planned to have dinner together somewhere far from army mess after Rick had his first round within the sacred precincts, I tagged along.

When we stepped into what you might call the anteroom at headquarters, the first thing we saw was the WAAC. She was sitting at a desk and her voice, talking United States over the telephone, was the swellest music we had heard in a long time. She was okay, too—no glamour girl—not many of those seem to have joined the WAACS—but she was nice. To us, she was beautiful. When she hung up and looked at us inquiringly, she gave us a quick smile but she was all business. Rick announced himself and she said, "Oh, yes, sir. The general is expecting you, sir."

She pushed the switch of the interoffice phone on her desk and said, "Captain Hallon reporting, sir," and then, to Rick, "Go right in, sir." All very military. She looked a question at me so I put on my best grin and said, "I'm just along for the ride."

She said, "Yes, sir. Won't you be seated, sir?" turned to

some papers on her desk and that was that. I was seated, sir.

She ignored me so completely I had a good chance to look her over. Her hair was on the reddish side, thick and wavy, but, of course, cut short according to WAAC regulations. Her mouth was nice and her eyes were a very deep blue. Her nose was short and pert and there was a sprinkling of freckles across the bridge and under her eyes. She was cute. I was glad I had come. So, after a couple of minutes, I tried. She hadn't looked at me once in the meantime.

"The weather," I said, feeling bright and original, "doesn't seem to be much better here than around Medjez-el-Bab," letting her know first shot I was a seasoned old combat veteran. I wondered hopefully if she had noticed my limp when I came in.

She looked up for nearly half a second and said, "Isn't it, sir?"

I said, "No." Strike one.

She went at her papers again, then glanced over at me and saw my mouth was opening for another try. A ghost of a smile like the one she had given us first seemed to pass over her face but it vanished and then her features became as expressionless as her voice as she started a monologue, sounding just like a copybook.

"I am Third Officer Elizabeth Ware, sir. My home is in Cleveland, Ohio. I have been in service six months. I trained with the first contingent of the Women's Army Auxiliary Corps at Fort Des Moines. I arrived in England in November. I was assigned to duty here two weeks ago. I came by plane. I like being in service very much. I am thrilled at being overseas, especially here. Excuse me, sir."

Her telephone had rung and she answered it. When she hung up again, I said, "Thank you," very humbly, then, "I haven't been asked so often, so I haven't a prepared speech and maybe you don't want to know anyway but I'm First Lieutenant Jim Kennard, United States Field Artillery. I was a reserve officer and was called into service two years ago. I don't remember anything before that. And you forgot something."

She said, "Yes, sir?" Cool, indifferent and a little bored.

"Yes, ma'am," I said, "you forgot to tell me when you will be off duty and if your friends call you 'Betty.' "

"My *friends* do—when I am off duty, sir," she said with just the right emphasis to put me in my place. She answered the telephone again, made a notation on one of the papers before her, laid it aside and turned to me of her own accord.

"Is Captain Hallon the one who used to play end for West Point?" she asked. That told me where I stood, too.

"Yes," I said. "That's how I met him."

"Oh," she said, "did you play for West Point, too, sir?"

I said to myself, "There's fame for you, Kennard," but to her I said, "No—against it."

She said, "Oh," and the conversation quietly folded up and died on its face. Strike two.

Still, you can't be shot for trying, so I heaved another forward pass. "Look, Miss Third Officer," I said, "please don't judge us too harshly. We haven't even seen an American girl for three months, much less talked to one. Most of the time we haven't seen any girls of any nationality, especially lately. You are a sight for bloodshot eyes and your voice is balm to the soul. Could you—" and just then Rick came out of the inner office. He seemed to be thinking about something weighty but not too deeply to take a good look at the WAAC. He half-bowed to her as he passed her desk and she gave him the full business of her smile.

"Miss—I mean Third Officer Ware," I said, "may I present Captain Richard Hallon, also of the United States Field Artillery. Rick—Third Officer Elizabeth Ware. She's from Cleveland. She's been in service six months. She was the first WAAC to get off the train at Fort Des Moines. She's been overseas since November. She came here two weeks ago by plane and she's thrilled. She likes the service, too. Her *friends* call her Betty—when she's off duty." I expected her to throw the telephone at me by this time but she didn't. She was giggling, so I went ahead. "I was just in the act of asking her to take pity on a couple of sex-starved soldiers and have dinner with us."

"Having any luck?" Rick asked.

"She likes West Point football players," I said. "Do your stuff."

At that she did flush a little but she laughed again. It was a very nice laugh. Rick faced her and straightened to attention. "Lieutenant Kennard and Captain Hallon respectfully request the pleasure of having Third Officer Ware as their guest at dinner this evening," he said.

She looked us both over, hesitated a moment, then stood up and saluted smartly. After we both had returned the salute, she said, "Third Officer Ware accepts, sirs."

Well, that was the beginning of it and things went faster and farther than any of us expected. She had had the same effect upon both of us and it never occurred to either of us to ask if she had a friend to make it a foursome. She appeared in a dinner frock—that still was permissible then for WAACS after office hours—and that really bowled us over. She looked gorgeous. She was about five feet six and just nicely rounded, not too slim and not plump. The WAACS don't go in for skinny girls. They have to have the physical stamina to take it. Her complexion was clear and fine and she had that radiant sort of health which the WAAC training gives them.

We ate and she and Rick danced—my leg wouldn't let me try that night, much as I wanted to—and we listened to the music and before the evening was over it was "Betty" and "Rick" and "Jim" all around.

Rick said we wouldn't be going back for four days and that made it swell. Before that first evening ended we told

Betty we were the two most selfish persons in the army but would she go out with us every night we were in Algiers? She didn't try to be coy about it. She wasn't the type. She just laughed and said she would.

She never intimated anything about it but she must have done some fast date cancelling for our benefit. A girl like her couldn't help but be popular and have her evenings booked pretty well in advance. Also we were conscious of dirty looks from other officers which were not hard to interpret.

We told Betty that since the holidays had been only calendar numbers to us, we would have to pretend the next night was New Year's Eve. She agreed and we took her to a shindig which was about as hilarious as was possible in a combat zone with a perpetual blackout and frequent air alarms. Keeping up the New Year's idea—as a matter of fact, this was the object of it—we both kissed Betty at midnight. What it did to me was terrific. I felt it right down to my shoes.

But the war was still on and, after midnight, it was just the beginning of another working day, so, half an hour later, we delivered Betty to her quarters.

The next night the three of us were together again. Betty and Rick did most of the dancing but I had rested practically all day so I ventured a couple of rounds with her and tried to look interestingly pale the rest of the time. But Betty was as impartial as the Articles of War. For every dance she had with Rick, she sat one out with me.

Once, while Rick was dancing with some other girl, Betty said to me, "You and Rick are rather close friends, aren't you?"

"Yes," I said. I didn't know what else to say so I didn't try.

She gave me an odd look, then said, "He seems to be a grand guy."

I said, "No, he isn't. He's the grandest guy. There's only one of him."

She gave me another quick look, then said, "He told me how you met."

"Oh," I said. My dialogue certainly was sparkling but I couldn't think of anything to add.

Then she gave me that smile of hers. "I think maybe you're wrong about him, though," she said. "I think maybe there *is* another one like him." She gave me her smile again and when I tumbled to what she meant, I wanted to say a lot of things but I didn't. I knew how Rick felt about her and I knew just as certainly that he hadn't been trying to make any hay while he was dancing with her so that stopped me, now.

Late that night, after we were back in our room and getting ready to turn in, Rick brought it up.

"You think a lot of Betty, don't you?" he said.

"I'm crazy about her," I said, "just as you are."

He grinned and said, "That's right. *The* girl, Jim?"

"The only one there ever was," I said, "and it isn't the war or loneliness or being away from girls a long while, either."

He grinned again. "Me, too," he said. "I certainly never thought I'd go for a girl in a uniform but here it is. Well, Jim, she's one thing we can't share forever."

"That's if she'll have either of us," I said. "Maybe we're a little too optimistic. She'll probably say 'no' twice—once to you and once to me."

He shook his head. "That's too simple a way out," he said. "Something tells me one of them will be 'yes.' "

All of a sudden, we were looking each other squarely in the eyes, looking for something we both found. Then we were grinning at each other and we both knew this wasn't going to make any difference between us, no matter how it turned out.

"So what do we do about it?" I asked.

"Wish each other luck and hope it doesn't work," he said and he was laughing.

So, on our last night in Algiers, it was just as it had been the other three nights except that we all felt sorry that it was the last night. We were just finishing dinner when I sprang it.

"Look, Betty," I said, "I don't like to inject a serious note into our final party but, once in a while, we have to face the facts of life and since we don't know when we'll all have a chance to be together again, this has to be said."

She looked at me in surprise and her smile was uncertain and Rick suddenly began staring at me oddly. He didn't know anything about this.

"It's like this," I said. "We haven't known you very long but sometimes that isn't necessary. Rick and I know you so well by now that we are both crazy about you. We're both in love with you. Both of us want to marry you. We're only sorry there aren't two of you, exactly alike but the world isn't that lucky. This is no time for fellows in our spot to ask anyone to marry them. But we want you to know we're both going to ask you when the right time comes. That's right, isn't it, Rick?"

He said, "That's right," and his face was all right again.

Betty just looked from one to the other of us. At first she smiled a little as if she thought it was a gag. Then she saw we meant it and her face went scared and white. Then, all of a sudden, there were tears in her eyes and, after that, just as suddenly, she came up with that real smile of hers, the softest, loveliest smile you ever saw. And then she said,

"You do mean it, and I'm very proud and happy but—you two—I couldn't bear it if I came between you."

"Do you think you could?" Rick asked sort of gently.

She looked at him for a long time, then looked at me just as long and then she shook her head and smiled again.

"No," she said and there was something almost breathless about the way she said it, "I couldn't. I don't think anyone or anything could." Her smile and her eyes suddenly became impish. "So then," she said, "I can go right ahead and fall in love with either one of you, without worrying, can't I? You know, the idea has rather tempted me."

"When you do get down to cases," Rick said, "remember that Jim's a pretty good bargain. I can recommend him."

"Personally," I said, "I think Rick would do a swell job of making a girl happy."

Betty started that soft laugh of hers. "Did either of you ever hear of John Alden?" she said and then we all laughed and whatever tension there had been was gone. Then she said, "You're sure neither of you is going to propose tonight?"

"Our word of honor," said Rick, grinning.

"Then we don't have to worry about it any more now, do we?" she said. "But," her voice became very stern and military, "don't forget you are officers and gentlemen and have given your word that you will—sometime," but her eyes were soft and warm when she said it. Then she said, "Sirs, may I have the pleasure of this dance with one of you?"

I couldn't help feeling a twinge when it seemed to me her eyes flickered toward Rick for a moment and it was with Rick she danced that one. But I stumbled through the next one with her and she was as impartial as ever.

Then, before we knew it, it was time to go home and we were saying good-bye and being much gayer about it than we felt. At the last moment, Betty kissed each of us and it didn't seem very impersonal, so each of us had something to take with us and remember. I still remember it.

\*

# XII

OUR WAR WAS STILL stuck in the mud when we went back to it, but we were there only one day when the orders came for the combat team to pack up and pull out. Rick said we were heading for central Tunisia where some other American troops already were in action, as much action as the weather permitted. We didn't know what we were going into but any shift was welcome, even if it only meant hopping from one mud bath into another.

As a matter of fact, that's about what it amounted to at first, although central Tunisia is distinctly different from the country we had left. The whole region is a high plateau, criss-crossed by jagged mountain ranges. The valleys between them are generally broad and flat. The soil is more sandy than in the north and dries out faster but it makes good mud when it's wet. Farther south, toward the salt lakes, the country becomes a desert. There are three principal passes through the mountains that separate the region from the coastal plain. Faid Pass is one of these.

There were two schools of rumors as to what we were going to do there. One school said we were going to try to drive through the passes to the sea to cut off Rommel who was still retreating. The other school said Von Arnim had received so many reinforcements our job, at this time, was simply to block the passes and prevent him from coming through for a crack at us. As soon as we arrived, we leaned toward that idea.

The Americans who already were there had mopped up the Axis units—mostly Italians—which had been on our side of the passes. When we moved in, all our forces in that part of the country were strung across the entrances to the three passes. From what we could see, our lines were pretty thin, much too thin for an attack against any strong force. Besides, it wasn't attack weather. When it rained, central Tunisia was a sea of impassable mud. It made any kind of maneuvering practically impossible and, for tanks, it was hopeless.

So it looked like defense to us and we went back into the same rainy season routine as before, without much to relieve the monotony. What that siege did do was show me how much my feeling toward Betty was the real thing. I found myself thinking of her most of the time—how she looked and smiled and danced and talked and the things she said. I'll admit I wasn't very optimistic. From the first, I was sure Rick had the call and I couldn't see why not. Her letters convinced me even more. She wrote us both regularly, the kind of letters we could read to each other and did. To Rick she seemed to pour out all her cheerful comradeship but there was a curious restraint in the way she wrote me. Just the same, her letters were the bright spots of that period. The only other cheerful thing I can remember about it was Byrnes' receiving his captain's bars.

Then the weather began to improve. The rains were shorter and the sun was out longer. The mud slowly hardened and all along the front the feeling grew that it wouldn't be long now. Then it was the middle of February and when General Eisenhower made a personal inspection of our positions, we were convinced something was going to break. Something did, all right, sooner than we expected, only it wasn't we who carried the ball.

The day it happened started out as one of the quietest we had had on our sector. There was a good deal of firing off in the distance somewhere to our right but nothing was happening where we were. Then, without any warning, the Jerry artillery opened up on us with everything they had.

Our observation post was on a narrow ridge which jutted

out into no man's land for quite a distance. Sommers' company was in position about two hundred yards back and three hundred to the right of us. A good many shells were dropping over there. Some of them burst near us but these seemed to be strays.

Through our binoculars, we could see a lot of movement across the way that had the earmarks of attack. When I called Rick to tell him trouble seemed to be coming, he said the gun crews were set for action as soon as we gave them some targets to work on. He said a lot of enemy shells were going over the battery positions but they hadn't hit much of anything yet.

The Jerry artillery fire seemed to increase with every minute and now, unmistakably, we could see their infantry coming out of their positions and edging into no man's land. Then Warren crawled over and pointed to the left, saying he had spotted tanks coming out of the Jerry lines over there. When I tried to call in the information, the line had gone dead. Wills went out on it and I used the remote control to give the FDC the news.

I couldn't get a good look at the tanks from where we were, so I scrambled ahead along the slope of the ridge until I was near the end of the remote control cable. Then I climbed up until I reached a good spot in a cluster of fair-sized rocks on something of a peak.

My first look from there didn't cheer me up. Tanks were breaking out from the enemy positions all the way across the sector, swinging out in front of the mass of infantry which was moving in right behind them. When I called the FDC and told them the worst, the S-3 said every forward observer and liaison officer on the front was calling for all available artillery and it was all going into action.

I reported the spread, range and pace of the tanks in our zone and the one-o-fives and mediums began pitching shells but even when the Long Toms joined in, it didn't add up to nearly enough fire power for this job. It just exposed our weakness.

Our fire was hitting among the tanks and we were wrecking a few of them but the rest came zigzagging along as if they knew we didn't have enough stuff to stop them. And that tidal wave of infantry behind them was growing bigger every minute as more and more of them came out of the Jerry positions, a lot more than we had on our side in this sector.

Barney cut in to tell me Wills had been back but before he could extend the line my way, it had gone out again and he was away on that repair job now. So I stayed with the remote control.

The doughboys rushed up with their antitank weapons and began to let fly with all they had, doing a good deal of damage but it still wasn't enough and the tanks kept rolling our way.

When they reached our ridge, they simply divided and cut past it on both sides, their guns going full blast. I could see what was left of the antitank outfits pulling back.

The Jerry infantry was coming within range now and Sommers' men began pumping away with their rifles and machine guns. Then the infantry was across no man's land, too, and one swarm of them headed for Sommers' position while another struck at our left company. The fighting around Sommers became heavier and heavier but I was so busy with the artillery fire on the tanks I couldn't watch what was happening back there.

I don't know how long it was before there seemed to be something queer about the firing around Sommers. When I looked back, I could see the reason. The company had fallen back at least three hundred yards. Then I saw Wills heading toward me with the telephone wire. The next second a shell burst almost directly in front of him. When the smoke cleared, he wasn't moving any more. He just lay crumpled on the ground.

I saw Warren crawl out to him and turn him over. He looked up toward me and shook his head. He made no move to help Wills, just took the chest reel from his shoulders and fumbled in his pocket for the splicing tools. Watching him, I felt rather hollow. I knew the detail had had its first fatality.

Warren clamped the telephone instrument to the wire for a quick test, then came crawling toward me as fast as he could, unreeling wire as he came. He flopped among the rocks beside me, out of breath but he connected the instrument for the test and handed the phone to me. He just said, "Don is gone, sir," but there was a lot of misery in his eyes. Then Barney called on the remote control and asked for Warren. I called through to the FDC on the telephone and while I was talking, Jack spoke to Barney for a few seconds, then dropped the remote control and hustled away.

By this time a good many of the tanks had passed us and when I looked back, the enemy infantry was closing in on Sommers. I told the FDC but the doughboys had to be on their own. Even with all the artillery we had working on the tanks, we weren't stopping them.

Then I saw Jack and Barney crawling up with the radio. We were practically surrounded already with the Jerry infantry behind us and their tanks on both sides of the ridge.

A shell burst almost in my ears but I was on my face and didn't get a scratch. When I looked up, I saw the hole, a big one, less than twenty feet away. The concussion had me dopey for a while and the next thing I knew, Johns and Warren had tumbled into the new shell hole. Barney looked my way grinning and yelled, "They dug this one just for us."

Maybe we should have gone back when the doughboys pulled out of their forward position but this was a perfect spot for directing fire on the tanks and the conformation of the ground was such that nobody could see us unless they stumbled our way which was unlikely. Our perch was practically an island and the Jerries had every reason to think there wasn't an American left around there. Now that we had the radio set with us, there wasn't a thing to indicate our presence except the telephone wire which wasn't very visible and even if a Jerry tripped over it, he'd probably feel sure it wasn't in use.

Just how much good all this was going to do us was doubtful because by that time, we couldn't have gone back if we'd wanted to. The Jerry tanks were past us on both sides of the ridge and the Jerry infantry was behind us. We heard the sounds of a terrific battle going on back there and knew it was Sommers' men fighting for their lives against overwhelming numbers.

The tanks weren't escaping damage. We were knocking some of them out but there were too many of them. Then Rick cut in to say, "Haven't you moved?"

I told him we hadn't had time. He said we must be back of the enemy and I said we were and the view was wonderful. Then he asked if we could get through and when I told him not unless they pushed the tanks back, he yelled, "For God's sake, how did you let that happen?"

"So you *could* push them back," I said, "business hasn't been very good so far."

"It will be," he said, "or *we're* going to move—in a heluva hurry."

"Then stop 'em," I said, "we don't think we'd like Jerry chow."

"Okay," he said, "here come the works."

He wasn't fooling. The fire on the tanks became heavier. The roar was tremendous and, up in our crow's nest, we held our breath. And now, for the first time, the tanks seemed to be having trouble.

Then it dawned upon us that the infantry fighting seemed to have stopped and next we saw something which made us sick. All that was left of Sommers' company was marching up, disarmed, between enemy guards. We could see Sommers at the head of them, a bandage around his head and his left arm bloody. That whole company knew where we were and finally passed not more than fifty yards away but not one of them so much as turned his head or batted an eye in our direction. We burrowed deeper in our holes and prayed for luck. We had it. Not a Jerry headed our way.

When they were past and we could look up again, we let out a yell. The whole fleet of enemy tanks had turned around and was streaking back. I told Rick what was happening and told him to keep on upping the range. Then we had to burrow again because all the Jerry infantry seemed to be headed for home again, too, but our luck held and we weren't spotted.

The tide had turned so quickly we were puzzled. We kept saying there was something wrong with this picture. Our artillery fire had not been heavy enough to cause this headlong retreat. Then we saw what we thought was the real cause —our own tanks, a lot of them, rolling fast.

We had just upped the range again when a burst of enemy shell fire dropped on our hill. Maybe it was just for luck or to make sure no damaging observation was coming from the peak but it killed the telephone and, since the way back seemed open again, Warren went out on the repair job.

Down below us everything looked good. The enemy tanks were back at their own positions but kept right on going as far as we could see. Through the binoculars, the leading elements of the enemy infantry seemed to be fading back with them, while our own tanks kept speeding up. It was entirely too good to be true and that something which had been buzzing in the back of my mind before started again but it didn't crystallize into anything except worry.

Through my glasses, I tried to look behind the forward enemy positions, for some clue as to what all the funny business was about. I thought I saw something but the angle wasn't good and I wasn't sure. Two or three hundred yards ahead of us was another point we couldn't reach before, which I thought might offer a better view. I took the remote control and started for it, yelling at Barney that I was going. I had the sudden feeling that it was urgent and ducked ahead in a sort of crawling run. Looking back, I saw Barney coming after me on the gallop. I didn't know what it meant but I needed him on the set and I stopped to signal him to go back. He told me later he thought I had called to him to go with me. That misunderstanding saved his life.

He understood my signal and started back. Before I went ahead again, I took another look through the binoculars and found I had a view through a gap in the hills. The few Jerries I could see looked suspiciously as if they were at gun positions. And, all of a sudden I got it. We had heard that Rommel had sent some of his troops up here to help guard his retreat to the north. This whole blitz today had been in the technique of Rommel, not Von Arnim. The thing I had been trying to remember was how Rommel had used exactly the same tactics against the British in Libya long before, attacked, then retreated until he had sucked in the British tanks within point-blank range of his eighty-eights and then had blown them to hell. He was trying the same trick again and we were falling for it, hook, line and sinker.

I raised the remote control phone to call Rick and give the warning just as an enemy salvo banged down on the perch where we had been. Barney hadn't reached it yet which was what saved him. He was down on his face and, for a moment, I thought he had been hit but he got up on his hands and knees and scrambled for his radio shell hole. He flopped into it and I tried again to call through but nothing happened. Then Barney showed his head and shoulders and made a signal which told the worst. The radio was out.

I thought I was going out of my mind while I scrambled back. Our tanks were rolling hell bent straight into the mouths of those waiting guns and with our telephone out, the radio was the only way to send through a warning that might have a chance to stop them. Barney was almost crying when I reached him. One of the Jerry shells had smashed his set to bits.

For the first time since we had been in combat, we were without direct communications to the battery or anyone else back there. I never felt so hopelessly helpless and did the only thing I could think of. I told Barney to hustle back to where he could wigwag a message. If Warren were back there, he would relay it or somebody else would. We had no flags with us, so Barney ripped his handkerchief in two and tied the pieces to a couple of splinters of his broken radio cases which would serve as sticks. Then he went back on the double.

I made a couple of flags for myself the same way, then climbed on top of a boulder and started wigwagging toward our tanks passing below, hoping somebody in one of them would see me. I kept repeating the same signals over and over. "Stop. Trap ahead. Stop. Trap ahead." But it was no use. Even if they saw me they probably thought it was a Jerry pulling a fast one.

I still was trying when our tanks walked into it. It was murder. They rolled right into the muzzles of the concealed eighty-eights and all I could do was stand by and watch tank after tank blown to bits or burst into flames or just stop, wrecked. Those in the rear tried to turn back but the eighty-eights seemed to be everywhere. I don't know how many tanks we lost altogether that day but it was a sickening few which escaped in our zone.

We didn't have to wonder what would happen after that and it came quickly. Rommel's tanks boiled out of the hills again and this time they looked like a tidal wave while with them came everything and everybody else the Jerries had, straight over the terrain they had crossed before but with a lot less to worry about this time.

There was nothing left for me to do where I was and I knew I'd have to step on it to get back at all. I found Warren and Johns just beyond where Sommers' company had been captured. Barney was badly wounded and Warren was trying to hold him up and take him to the rear. He had been hit by a shell fragment just after he had wigwagged his message to Jack who had relayed it and then gone to help Barney. The message went through too late to do any good, of course, but, at least, we had tried.

Barney was practically out and we had a difficult time moving him. The whole terrain was hashed up, torn up by shellfire with more coming over all the time. Battle debris was littered everywhere—rifles, helmets, wrecked machine guns, not to mention the bodies of both Americans and Jerries. There was some confusion among the doughboys we ran into. They had arrived too late to help Sommers' company, had tried to establish a new position and now had been ordered back again. We did manage to find a couple of litter bearers who started Barney on his way to the hospital. Then Warren and I headed for the spot where our jeep had been parked. All we found was the wreck of it. It looked as if somebody had tossed a couple of hand grenades into it, maybe one of our own doughboys, to keep it from being captured. There wasn't anything worth salvaging.

We hurried on back to the battery position but the battery wasn't there any more. The whole battalion had pulled out—and just in time. Rommel's forces were pouring ahead like a flood and smashing straight through our lines. We didn't have much time to get away ourselves and we might not have made it if a reconnaissance car hadn't come along and picked us up.

When we finally reached the battery which had taken up a new position away back, Rick looked at us as if he didn't believe it. He said, "My God, out of the grave again. How many rabbits' feet do you carry?" But we didn't have time to talk. The battery was firing as fast as it could pump out the shells. Rick told us that, while Sommers' company was the only outfit lost in our zone, a lot of the left battalion had been captured, including the FO and two members of the Battery B detail and our liaison officer. For fire direction, the battalion was depending almost entirely on messages which came through from retreating doughboys who had escaped the first rush.

That meant Warren and I had to go back to work. We commandeered one of the battery's other radio sets and started forward again. We didn't have to wonder where to go to find targets. It was just straight ahead. We could hear the Jerries with no trouble and they were more than willing to meet us halfway.

# XIII

I HOPE WE NEVER have to go through another nightmare like the one that started that day. Rommel made us look pretty bad. Not only had we fallen for a trick which already had been blueprinted for us but all the other things which were wrong with us began to show up in a hurry, particularly the results of our lack of discipline and co-ordination.

The carelesssness about security was particularly costly. I hate to think about what happened to some of those boys who found it too much trouble to dig a foxhole and had nothing but slit trenches to fall into when Rommel's tanks came rolling through. Those tank drivers loved slit trenches with Americans in them. They would run their treads right into the trench, then half turn—like a meat grinder. No, it isn't pretty to think about but it happened to too many of our men. It couldn't have happened if they had been in fox holes. And there just wasn't the co-ordination between the artillery and infantry and air forces we should have had and which could have done a lot to prevent or stop what was happening now.

When Jack and I started back that day, we were about as depressed as we thought possible then. We were getting the pants licked off us, we had had our first man killed and Barney was badly wounded with Furman already in the hospital. Besides that, we were moving forward against a tide of retreating doughboys, so it seemed we were heading straight into worse trouble than we had had before, except that Rick had given us strict orders to avoid capture. In case it looked as if they were closing in on us, we were to duck.

Handling an army on the attack is a stiff enough job but it's a picnic compared with a retreat. There were no white feathers in that army of ours but there was a hellish lot of confusion. Actually, I guess we handled ourselves better than we had any right to. In all the mix-up, there was no panic. For the most part, the men were sore as goats, which is a good sign for an army being kicked in the teeth. They just wanted to get set for the chance to slug back.

This wasn't easy, just then, not under the speed with which Rommel struck and kept striking. We lost a good many men and a lot of equipment so that it constantly seemed more difficult to make a stand which would be effective.

On that first jump back to the forward zone, Warren and I didn't have far to go before things became thick. In fact, we weren't up more than a mile and a half before we saw the tanks rolling our way. When we had the radio planted in something like a defilade, the first message to Rick was a warning that the battalion had better prepare to move back again. But Rick said, "Not yet," and our fire missions were accepted. The artillery was plenty willing. It knocked out some more of the tanks but our fire power wasn't enough to do more than make the rest a little more cautious but they kept on coming.

We had to pull back half a mile, then another half mile and then we were almost at Rick's OP, moving back with a thin line of doughboys, retreating but still pitching everything they had. It was growing dark, now, which helped. It gave the battalion a chance to pull up stakes again and the doughboys to try to establish some kind of defense positions. But we didn't have enough men or stuff available to do more than slow Rommel down. Until we had plenty more, it didn't look good.

It wasn't good. Rick told me the battalion was going back eight thousand yards with nobody expecting the new positions to be the last stopping place in that direction. There was no sleep for us. All night long, the Jerry infantry and artillery kept punching away at us to prevent us from getting squared away to meet the renewal of the main attack in the morning. By daylight, we had staggered back another half mile and our hows weren't much more than seven thousand yards back.

The one break we had was the arrival of Byrnes and his company up where we were. Somehow, things always seemed to improve with Byrnes around. This night, when we certainly needed any sort of lift, was no exception. He slapped back one Nazi punch without our help and then smelled out another, bigger one and gave us such accurate information that when we called in the fire missions, our hows were on the targets so fast they smashed the enemy formations before they were within hailing distance of our lines.

After that, we weren't bothered for a couple of hours and Byrnes and I had a reunion. He had been out with a minor wound and we hadn't seen each other for a couple of weeks. We spent most of our time talking about ways and means to improve methods of operation between forward observers and the infantry. We both agreed neither the infantry nor the artillery had the right system yet for making the best use of FOs, especially so far as continual contact between the FO and the leading elements was concerned. We evolved several ideas for strengthening the setup but it was just wishful conversation that night. We knew we had bigger worries right in our laps than changes in the FO routine.

It seems now as if the chat we had that night was the last time I stopped moving during the whole sickening retreat we had just begun. Byrnes kept on doing brilliant work, making the Jerries pay for every foot they pushed ahead, though you could hardly figure in terms of feet when Rommel was pounding forward six and seven miles a day. But Byrnes had only one company and his good work was just a drop in the bucket. The company suffered a lot of casualties. After two days of retreat, retreat, retreat, it was down to a handful and had to be relieved.

There seemed to be no end to it. The Jerries kept coming—fast—and they wrecked our center. They sliced through and were pushing us back and back until it looked as though we would be shoved all the way out of Tunisia and back into Algeria.

It was discouraging and humiliating but, more than that, it was fantastic. At that time, Rommel was supposed to be a beaten dog. Instead, here he was slapping us around like schoolboys and moving so fast we couldn't get set anywhere to block him.

During the first night, Rick sent us a new telephone man, Phil Renburg, who introduced himself by handing me the telephone in the dark and telling me the line had been checked and was okay. Next day, Rick sent us Dan Drake, to replace Barney. Both were good men in their own lines though they had had no training in forward observer work. They had to work into it on the run as there was no time to teach anybody anything. They were willing and that was all we could ask just then.

Renburg hadn't been with us an hour before Rommel's force started driving again. From that minute, we didn't know what it meant to rest or sleep. None of us ever had worked so hard in our lives or under such terrific pressure. We couldn't let up at all. The enemy kept slugging and then slugging some more. Our forward observing consisted chiefly of reporting their pace and progress and the forces Rommel was throwing into the fight. We directed plenty of fire missions but the amount of artillery we had couldn't do more than slow down the attack a little. The battalion had to be ready to pack up and move back again any minute.

All of us were becoming exhausted. Personally, I was climbing up and down hills and crawling through gullies or scrambling across half-open country from morning till night and from night till morning. My eyes became bleary and bloodshot. My legs were like shafts of lead and they were so wobbly sometimes I thought they would cave under me.

Dolan was wounded the second day of the retreat. That meant there was no chance of relief because, God knows, Rick had his hands full. At it was, he came up a couple of times for an hour or so and I took his place at the battery OP but I was so much on edge it was worse than being on the job up ahead. I practically had to force Warren, Drake and Renburg to snatch naps when they could and Warren spelled me for the few hours of sleep I did get. We all had forgotten what a warm meal was like.

Every man on the front was worn to a frazzle. Rommel had moved so fast and given us such a mauling we were in worse shape than even he knew. He had us where he could lash out to the north, south or west. The night we seemed to be having a breather, we knew in the back of our minds it was just an interlude before the worst blow sent our way yet, that it only meant Rommel was bringing up more stuff, and that it was up to us to make the most desperate stand we could with what we had left.

I didn't dare go to sleep. The very quiet made me suspicious. Once, a strong enemy patrol came over, so big we first thought it was an attack. There were enough of them to drive the doughboy outposts back and we had a merry little fight with them before we drove them off. I say "we" because the FO detail was in it and we had a chance to use our carbines for a few rounds. I was still carrying Furman's carbine. I hadn't packed my automatic since the day he had been wounded. After that we moved because there was no use staying in a spot the Jerries had located. From our new position, Warren and I went out after things became a little too quiet again. We ran into another patrol and had to move fast to avoid being captured.

Things went that way all night and, as soon as morning came, the pressure was on again and we stumbled back a little farther. But the blow wasn't as hard as we had expected and we had the chance to steady down. Then the firing became heavier off to our left and far ahead of us and the word came through that the Jerries were brushing past us for bigger game ahead. We tried to crowd back but we could not budge an inch beyond the line where Rommel apparently had decided to hold us while he went on his way.

Byrnes came back into the fight with about half the replacements he needed and kept trying to feel out the enemy, looking for a spot to land a blow which might help the fellows who were in that uproar beyond us. We were doing the same thing, dragging all over the zone, looking for something, anything we could transform into a break because the Jerries certainly weren't giving us any of their own free will.

Warren and I went out on a limb again and once more came within an eyelash of being captured. We managed to get away but it just about finished me. It was all the fast motion—or motion of any kind—I had left in me. I was dizzy from weariness. But you can always do what you have to do and I kept going for just that reason—I had to.

All along our sector, the doughboys were fighting and the artillery was firing almost continuously but we couldn't dent the Nazi line. I wondered how things were going off to our left where the real battle was going on, wondered in a dull sort of way because I didn't seem able to think about anything much except what was directly in front of me.

It was about fourteen hundred when I saw Rick coming up and wondered how he could move so fast and what he was doing up here. Then there was a mission to handle and I was adjusting fire when he scrambled up beside me.

"I'll take over," he said. "Go back and get some rest. I've been having it soft at the OP. Handle it for a while."

I said, "Not a chance. I'm all right."

"You're out on your feet," he said. "Go on back. That's an order."

Just then Jerry machine guns began blazing away in our direction and shells began plunking around us, so all we could do was hug the ground, the racket so loud and continuous we couldn't even talk. When it subsided a little, I tried to argue with Rick but he gave me a shove to start me on my way. "Go on back," he said again. He took an envelope from his pocket and handed it to me. "Here's a letter from Betty which just came for you," he said. "I have one, too. We'll compare notes later. We're going away from here. We'll call you as soon as we're located."

I put the letter into my own pocket. For some reason, Rick put out his hand and I shook it. Then he grinned at me. "Have a nice vacation—for two hours," he said.

"I'll send you a postcard," I said. I didn't know how dopey I was until I was on my way. I was crawling back to the battery in my sleep. It was a good three thousand yards back from the observation point and all I remember is leaving the detail and then tumbling into Rick's foxhole at the battery OP.

An officer I hadn't met before was on duty. He said his name was Venner and he had come up the night before to replace Dolan. He was supposed to go back to duty as assistant exec when I came along but he didn't because I just passed out for a while. Not for long, though. It was only a little after fifteen hundred when I awoke and heard the telephone man making a check with Renburg so it went through my mind hazily that our line must have gone out and been repaired while I was dozing. I shook myself out of the fog and told Venner it was okay for him to leave now. When he was gone, it was compulsory for me to stay awake. I needed a pretty strong reason. Then a call came from Rick.

"New spot," he said. "Take it. Jig-Mike 76. Base point dead ahead. Six hundred."

It took a few seconds for that to percolate. Then I yelled, "Hey, what are you doing away up there?"

"Gangway, fire mission," he came back, cool as ice. "Base point two hundred left, four hundred short. Troop concentration. Will adjust."

From the FDC came the word, "Accepted" and then, "On the way."

"On target. Fire for effect," Rick said, "I must be getting good," and he laughed.

After that, nothing happened for a while and I settled down to luxury. All I had to do here was stand in the foxhole, lean on my elbows and watch the terrain ahead without moving. It was a little tough staying awake but I made it. Then Rick called again.

"I've moved," he said and chuckled. "Ran the wire myself while Renburg was fixing another break. Base point is one hundred right, four hundred over."

That really jolted me. He was practically in Rommel's lap.

"Rick," I called, "for the love of God——"

"View wonderful," he said. "Think I see something. Stand by."

I didn't know what to say. This had me jittery. Rick wasn't foolhardy. He was one of the most sensible persons I ever knew but in his new location, I didn't see how he could throw a rock in any direction without stirring up the Jerries. I couldn't even understand how he managed to reach it without being killed or captured. He wouldn't have taken that kind of chance without the most urgent reason, one so serious a great deal depended upon it.

Then, without warning, the enemy artillery opened up—on the forward zone, the doughboy reserve area, our howitzer positions, and the mediums behind us. It was the heaviest fire we had had since the day of the break through. The telephone man at the OP suddenly said, "FDC line out, sir," and jumped out on it. And then came Rick's voice.

"Fire mission," he said but I interrupted him.

"FDC line out," I said, "use radio."

"Can't," he said, "remote control out. Can't get to set. Relay it by radio—and fast." His voice was perfectly cool as he went on. "All artillery. Base point one hundred right, four hundred over. Many tanks. Hurry."

"Right," I said. I grabbed the radio—and then it hit me. "Rick!" I yelled, "that's your position. Give me right data."

"I did," he said. "Base point one hundred right, four hundred over. Hurry."

I felt as if I had turned to ice. "Rick," I shouted, "get out of there. I won't send in that mission until you're out."

"I have to stay," he said. "Only way to stop 'em. I smelled it. That's why I'm here. Send it in. That's an order. Hurry."

"I can't, Rick," I said. "I can't. Not to you."

"Fire mission," he said. "Send it. This is our one chance. For God's sake, don't spoil it. Make it worth while. Hurry."

"Rick!" I yelled again, "Rick, in the name of God——"

"Fire mission," he said. "Train on me. Hurry."

There are some things you have to do in war. I picked up the radio and called the FDC. "All artillery. Base point one hundred right, four hundred over. Tanks. Hurry."

"One hundred right, four hundred over," I heard the S-3 say. "Accepted. Stand by." I heard him repeat the directions and call for all the artillery. Then he gave some sort of exclamation and the next second he was saying to me, "Good God, you must be wrong. That's Captain Hallon's position."

I said, "Yes, sir. Data correct. Captain Hallon's order. This is Kennard. Hallon radio out. Am relaying."

For a moment, he was silent, then his voice came over, as dead as my own, "On the way."

The radio man at the OP was standing in his foxhole, looking at me, as rigid as if he'd been made of stone. He had heard what was going on, even in that hellish din. Finally he said, "Better get down, lieutenant," and, for the first time, I realized I had climbed out of my own foxhole and was standing up, staring at the terrain ahead. I dropped on my knees. God knows, if ever I wanted to pray, it was then.

It was hot that day, damned hot, but I was shivering when I slid back into the foxhole with the telephone glued to my ears. I stood there shaking through the seconds until the sound of the bursts came—at least, I thought they were our bursts—and with them came Rick's voice.

"Short one hundred," he said, his voice as calm as ever. "Fire for effect. Keep it there. Make it thick and they won't get through."

Into the radio I mumbled, "Short one hundred. Fire for effect." Another fifteen seconds and all twelve hows of the battalion roared.

Rick's voice came again, "On. Keep there."

The mediums and the heavies came in and more one-o-fives from the right and left and then it was Rick's voice once more, "So long, Jim. It's been swell."

I'm not ashamed that I was crying when I said, "So long, Rick," but he never heard me. The line was dead.

I just stood there, stunned, while our heavies joined in. Rick had asked for "all artillery." We were giving him all we had. I don't know how long it lasted. It seemed forever. I felt dizzy. I wanted to yell for the guns to stop. But in a war you just do what you have to and whatever hits your chin, you take.

The radio man called me. I picked up the remote control phone. It was Warren. His voice was shaky. "Mission accomplished," he said. "Tanks stopped. Many smashed. Others falling back. Captain Hallon—I'm afraid, sir."

I guess I went a little crazy. I called Venner and I must have sounded hysterical. "Come up here," I yelled. "I've just killed Captain Hallon. I'm going up."

As soon as I saw him coming, I waved at the OP and I was on my way. I didn't even bother to duck. I just ran and scrambled my way up there. It wasn't until I saw the wrecks of some of the tanks and spotted Warren, Drake and Renburg crouched close together among them that I realized I would endanger their lives if I kept on exposing myself, so I flopped and crawled up the rest of the way.

They had found Rick. He probably had been killed the moment he said good-by. He couldn't have escaped. Our fire had torn up every inch of the terrain. And when I reached there and looked down at him, all I could think was that this was my handiwork.

I don't remember much of what happened the rest of that day. We were in an exposed position and the first thing we did was take Rick's body back as far as our doughboy positions. I couldn't even go back any farther with it. I had to work and keep on working.

It didn't take long to learn Rick had done more than stop a tank attack. He had saved us all from being trapped. That was why Rommel had driven past us in the morning and then turned to the left. The attack on us was to have cut through as the other prong of the pincers to lock us in a pocket. Rick must have sensed what was coming and he had taken the only possible way to stop the drive—smash it before it was well under way—by fire direction from a spot where he couldn't miss.

Rommel tried again, of course, almost immediately, but we were set for him this time and he had to give up on our zone but the fighting kept up there, hard, desperate fighting, while the Jerries rolled ahead beyond us on the left.

Somewhere along the line, I had a few minutes' breather and reached into my pocket for a cigarette. I came up with Betty's letter which I hadn't opened. I read it then. She had written it just a couple of days before, immediately after

Rommel's break through and there was worry in every line of it but one passage was like a slap in the face.

"So much of the safety of the battery depends upon your work," she wrote, "and that means Rick's safety, too. Take good care of him, Jim. But I know you will." It was the same as if she had written, "Take care of him for me." There hadn't been much doubt in my mind before. Now there was none. I had lost both of them in one day. I would have to write to her and what could I say? "Take good care of him." I had taken care of him, all right. I had killed him.

I went back to work. The war was still going on, even if a lot of things had stopped for me, just about everything there was for me, personally. All I had left was the war.

# XIV

"WHEN LIEUTENANT KENNARD came back to the detail, he was like a dead man walking," said Warren. "We worried about him a lot. Everything about him was as tight as a drum. He scarcely ever spoke except in line of duty. But he kept right on working. He practically never accepted any relief. He would let me spell him once in a while but he was always back on the job in about half an hour and it was easy to see he hadn't rested. I don't think he slept at all through all the rest of the time we were being pushed back.

"That seemed to go on forever although, actually, it was only about eight days altogether. In that time, we had retreated more than fifty miles. We had expected Rommel to be stopped at Kasserine Pass but he plowed right through it. We had our backs against the Algerian border and it looked as if we would be pushed across it right onto our big base at Tebassa. But Rommel swung away from us and turned north toward Sbiba.

"Then we heard that reinforcements had come down from the north, especially artillery, and had straddled his path. We could hear the sounds of very heavy firing over there and that night came word that Rommel had run into a stone wall but was still trying. The next day we moved back into position to join in. For the next two days the fighting was terrific and we were firing all the time. But it was swell. Rommel had been stopped in his tracks. You can imagine how we felt after the beating we had been taking. We had more planes on the job there than we had seen at any time before and they helped a lot but it was the artillery and the dough-boys who carried the load and broke Rommel's back.

"On that third day, when the one-o-fives and mediums

pulverized the Jerries' last tank attack, we knew the dog days were over. We were away up that day, on a hill where we had a swell view of the tanks being chewed up by our fire. Lieutenant Kennard was in a shell hole a few yards from the one in which Renburg and I were and when I looked over at him, it seemed as if all the tension was gone from his face. He glanced around at us with a funny kind of smile and waved toward where some Jerry infantry were being torn up by time shells.

" 'A very pretty sight,' he said. Then he pointed to where half a dozen Jerry tanks were burning. 'But there,' he said, 'is the noblest sight on God's earth—torches made of Mr. Rommel's tanks, each one full, I hope, of roasting Nazis, getting a taste of the hell where they all are going.' He laughed and said, 'I like the way war brings out all our finer instincts. I can remember away back when I was a human being.' Then he said, 'God, I'm tired. I could sleep for a week. Let's go to work.'

"So we knew everything was all right again."

It wasn't—exactly (Kennard went on again), but knowing we were beginning to pay off for Rick did loosen things up. When Venner came up with some men to relieve us that afternoon, we went back. Barrett, who was acting battery commander, told me to rest as long as I wanted to. When I lay down, I didn't awaken until about noon next day. When I reported to Barrett, he told me the fight which had stopped Rommel was over and for me to get some more sleep while I could. I tried but it didn't work. Too many things were becoming real which had only seemed to be nightmares before. I finally sat down to write that letter to Betty which I had been dreading. I still didn't know what to say to her. Finally I did the only thing I could think of. I just wrote what actually had happened. When I finished that, I couldn't add a single word of comment. I just signed what I had written and sent it on its way. I never received a reply to that letter but I hadn't expected one. It seemed to put a period at the end of something even though I wasn't very successful in trying not to think too much about Betty.

From that time on, everything about the war seemed different. Things were pretty empty without Rick and that only grew worse as time went on because I never could get away from the realization that, no matter what the circumstances were, I had killed him. I kept thinking about how our friendship had begun, in that football game when Rick always said I had saved his life and how I now had ended it by causing his death. I had a close call from going completely morbid about it. It was always in the back of my mind but I tried to shake it off by working a little harder and trying to avoid shedding gloom around the fellows.

We still had our job to do. Before, it had all been personal. The most important thing had been what happened to me and the friends who were fighting alongside me. Now, I realized war didn't pay much attention to friendship. I didn't count, either. Nothing counted except winning the war. What we felt and thought and wanted as individual human beings didn't mean anything against that. Rick had realized that when I didn't. I kept thinking his death should have meant more than the stopping of one tank attack. Finally, it did—to us, at least.

He had been able to stop the tanks because he had gone up so far he couldn't help locating the right targets when it was most important and then could direct fire which couldn't miss at the time it would do the most good. It looked like a good pattern for forward observation—not to be suicidal as Rick had had to be but to get up there, farther than we ever had before, to do a better job. We already had been up pretty far ahead of the doughboys a couple of times, mostly by accident but we hadn't deliberately had observation posts as near the enemy as we could get. But we began to do that now. The fellows of the detail were all for it. You see, all of them had seen Rick killed.

Rommel was retreating now and we were headed east again, so we had good country in which to experiment with advanced forward observation. We had been over it before and we knew practically every hill and rock and wadi.

After that, we almost never had our observation posts behind the doughboys. Either we were right with them or away up ahead of them. Most of the time we were out front. The system worked. I wish we could claim exclusive credit for originating it but the fact is, the idea hit a lot of forward observers so that advanced observation became the rule for the American artillery. The Jerries didn't like the results. Prisoners told us the deadliness of American artillery fire was becoming the worst hell on the front.

There seems to be a sort of inevitable continuity about things, even in a war, a pattern which works out with cumulative results. If Rommel hadn't smashed through us and exposed our weaknesses, we might have gone muddling along and made a hash of things which would have prolonged the campaign for months. As it was, it only took us about two weeks to discover most of the things which were wrong with the setup.

One thing about Americans—we learn fast. It seemed almost as if we learned overnight when we started east again. From the time we stopped Rommel, our lessons seemed to take effect. For the first time, we began to have real co-ordination between the infantry and artillery and our air force support kept improving. Of course, we fumbled a good deal at first because we weren't used to it, yet, but we weren't just feeling our way around in the dark any more. Our operations began to be smarter and, every day, we knew how a little better until, when it came to the final job, we were all set.

The same thing was true of our forward observer detail. Everything seemed to dovetail, piece by piece. If we hadn't already learned the tricks necessary to take care of ourselves, we wouldn't have lasted a week with our advanced forward observation. And, being away out there in patrol territory inevitably led to the forward observer's going out with the infantry patrols at night, which gave us more information and strengthened the tie-in with the doughboy operations. And that, in turn, finally led to another change, under which the FO stayed with one doughboy outfit, instead of trying to spread-eagle a whole zone and have the doughboys hunt for him when they needed him in an emergency. That improved efficiency and co-ordination, too.

We had a good many casualties—more than I like to think about—but even they played their part. We learned to take them in our stride and shift or double up jobs automatically, so the work could go on without a break.

We only reached these phases step by step through a grind which never seemed to stop. After their first high-geared retreat to Faid Pass from Sbiba, the Jerries fought us every inch of the way. They had to, because Montgomery already was pushing the Afrika Korps up the coast. The Italians didn't give us much trouble. They always admitted early that they were licked and we captured a lot of them. But the Heinies were tougher and every time we reached them, it was a slugging match.

The chief reason we didn't crash through them in a hurry was the extent to which they peppered the country with land mines. They literally planted millions of them. The advance of the Second Corps was determined largely by the speed with which the engineers could clear the path with their mine detectors. In the Faid Pass area, they dug up as many as five thousand to the square mile, every one of them designed to blow up a tank.

This made it ticklish for the FO detail because we often couldn't wait for the engineers. But, one day, Warren showed up with a mine detector. I never asked him where he picked it up for fear I'd have to return it to the man who owned it. We just went ahead and used it and after that, we didn't have to be so skittish when we went up looking for an observation post. While he was at it Warren had learned how to handle the mines so when we spotted any, we could dig them up if necessary, without being blown to pieces.

As we pushed ahead, the fighting became heavier and the front began to be more irregular every day, so we were receiving calls for artillery fire from all sides and chasing all over to do the necessary observing. We were wishing there were more FOs or that the doughboys could adjust fire themselves sometimes.

As a matter of fact that did happen once. Barrett, who had his captain's bars now, was up front and I was at the battery OP. The enemy fire was heavy and made it one of those days when the FO telephone line was out constantly and, finally, even the radio went cold, so for a while we had no communications with the FO detail at all. It was during this that a strange voice came over the OP radio saying he was a doughboy lieutenant whose men were being held up by a battery of eighty-eights he had spotted and was there any chance to get some artillery fire on it? When I asked him if he could adjust fire, he said he didn't know how but I told him to try anyway. He didn't know anything about the base point or the gun-target line but he gave the location of the eighty-eights as best he could.

When I called the FDC, I was told to go ahead and try the job with Battery C as the rest of the battalion was needed on another mission. I told the doughboy lieutenant we would send a salvo out there and asked him to report how far we missed the target in yards and in what direction—north or south and east or west.

When the salvo hit, he said, "About three hundred yards west and two hundred south." I had the battery deflect five hundred yards to the right and upped the range four hundred, hoping to get a bracket on the eighty-eights. Then I told the doughboy the changes we were making so he would have a scale on the ground between the first and second salvos. He caught on and we got our bracket. The third round landed just short of the target. On the fourth, the sensing wasn't exactly according to the book. All I heard was, "Wow! Boy, oh, boy!" Then he came to and said, "You're right on 'em. Give 'em hell."

After that, while the battery was pouring it on, he nearly broke the radio with his yells and he kept saying, "How do you do it? Wow! I hardly told you anything and you can't even see 'em. Boy, oh, boy! How do you do it?" I finally broke through his whoops long enough to ask him to report when we had neutralized the eighty-eights. He yelled, "Hell, there's nothing left of 'em, now. Boy, oh, boy!"

So I called "Cease firing" but when I tried to get the doughboy again, he was gone, probably already on his way with his men. We learned later he had just been fishing around with his radio, hoping to catch some artillery and happened to tune in on us.

The best thing that happened that day, though, was the return of Furman, who showed up while I was still at the OP. He was a little pale but all in one piece and anxious to go back to work. So when Barrett called to say he was coming in, I asked him to bring Renburg along as Furman was going up with me.

Then we ran into a streak of bad luck. Two days later, Drake was killed while he was moving his radio from one observation point to another. A good operator, named Joe Sumner, came up to take his place. A couple of days after that, we hit rough going again with the Jerry artillery so active Furman was kept on the run, repairing the telephone lines every half hour. Finally, he had so many splices in the last five hundred yards of wire up to our observation post that the resistance was becoming too strong and he started back for new wire to replace that stretch.

While he was gone, I had a call from Byrnes that he wanted to see me. There wasn't too much defilade around there so I had to take a rather circuitous route to reach him. I had just rounded a hill about four hundred yards back when I was stopped in my tracks by what I saw. In front of me were nine dead Jerries, lying around three sides of a clump of rocks. Behind the rocks was another body—Furman. It was easy to see what had happened. He had been trapped by some Jerry patrol sneaking in from our flank and had managed to reach shelter behind the rocks. He must have accounted for all those dead Jerries alone because there wasn't a sign of another American around. Well, killing him had been expensive—but not expensive enough. I wouldn't have traded him for the whole damned Nazi army. He had been back from the hospital just four days.

Maybe I hadn't become as hard as I thought. From the time he had been wounded in that shell hole fight in the rain, I had carried his carbine. When he came back from the hospital, he had brought up a new one but I had traded with him. Now, his old carbine was lying beside his body and I traded back again. I wanted that one of his. I wanted to be able to think I was using it for him the next time I fired at a live target and I had a hunch I wouldn't miss.

Renburg came back to us that night but his stay was short. He was with us less than twenty-four hours, caught in the worst day we ever had for casualties. But that's Jack's story. I was one of the casualties. In fact, I was the first one.

"It started out as one of the best days we'd had," said Warren. "First the doughboys smashed the Jerries who had been holding us up the day before and they kept right on going. We were moving up to a new observation post every half hour or so and all Renburg had to do was string wire ahead, with never a repair job. Nothing the Jerries pitched seemed to bother the telephone lines. And since we didn't have time to dig foxholes, we just kept going from shell hole to shell hole.

"By the middle of the afternoon, Renburg had used all his wire and we were at the end of the line, so far as using the telephone was concerned, until the battery came up again. Then the lieutenant took the remote control and went out to adjust fire on a target we couldn't see from where we were. He had just disappeared around a hill up ahead of us when the telephone line went out for the first time and Renburg went out on it. The lieutenant adjusted on the target he went out for and was on his way back, still out of sight when he suddenly called through another fire mission on a machine-gun nest. Then he said he had spotted it by being hit himself and he asked Captain Barrett to send up a relief. I wanted to go and help him but he told Sumner he could make it to our shell hole all right.

"Just then I saw Renburg coming back, about two hundred yards away when a shell burst near him and I saw he was hurt. I hustled down to where he was. He was unconscious but his wound didn't look too serious and, after I had given him first aid, I took his tools and the telephone and checked the line and then found some litter bearers who took him away.

"When I reached our shell hole again, Lieutenant Kennard was there. A machine-gun bullet had slashed the fleshy part of his left arm and he had lost a lot of blood, so he was a little groggy. He had had a tough time tying up the wound, so I gave it a new bandage and wanted to get a litter for him but he said he would be able to walk it after he had rested a little.

"After a while, Lieutenant Venner came up. Lieutenant Kennard started back and we waited until we were sure he

could walk all right and then we started chasing the doughboys, who were pretty far ahead of us by now."

"When I reached the dressing station," Kennard inter-
jected, "the medic told me if I kept on getting punctured
like this, he was going to use me for a lawn sprinkler after
the war."

"We didn't have any communications except the radio,"
said Warren, "so we had to pack the set wherever we went,
which kept us hustling. Then the doughboys hit a snag and
we thought we were going to get up to them at last but a
runner came to say the doughboy captain wanted to see
our forward observer, so Lieutenant Venner told us to put
up the set in the nearest shell hole and get it ready while he
went up with the remote control. I paid out about four hundred yards of cable before he reached the captain. After they
had been talking a couple of minutes, the lieutenant began
to call in a fire mission but, just then, a lot of Jerry shells
crashed around them and the remote control went dead.

"When the smoke cleared, both the captain and Lieutenant Venner were down. I yelled to Sumner to pack up, we
were moving up there and had to take the set with us. The
Jerries were still firing so we spaced out about thirty yards
apart and hugged the ground as much as we could while we
went ahead. I couldn't see much up ahead but when we were
closer, I saw some doughboys there and one of them seemed
to be bandaging the captain.

"Some of the shells were dropping too close so I turned to
yell at Sumner to hurry when I saw he was stretched out and
wasn't moving at all. His radio case was about six feet from
him. When I reached him, he was out. His arm had been
broken and he had been hit in the leg, too. I gave him the
fastest first aid I could but I couldn't stay with him. Packing

both the radio cases, it seemed like an hour before I reached the lieutenant.

"There wasn't a scratch on him but he was out cold from the concussion. It must have knocked the remote control out of his hand because it was lying a dozen feet away, smashed to bits. Litter bearers had come up to get him and the captain. I told them about Sumner and they said they would take care of him.

"The Jerry fire was getting heavier and all the other doughboys were taking to cover. I just set up the radio in the nearest shell hole and was calling Captain Barrett to tell him what had happened and that I was the only member of the detail left when, in the distance, up ahead, I saw Jerry infantry and a few tanks heading our way in a counterattack.

"I stopped handing Captain Barrett my tale of woe and, instead, made a quick guess as to the range of the Jerries and sent in a fire mission. After that, there wasn't much to it. I just squatted in the shell hole and kept calling the range as the Jerries came closer. They were so strong that our doughboys pulled back to get a better defensive position but I had to reduce the range so fast and so often I hardly noticed them passing me. If I had, I probably would have gone back with them.

"Then I saw the battalion alone wasn't going to be able to turn the trick, so I asked for more artillery. I was lucky. They turned the mediums and heavies loose on the zone. I had pulled down the range to about a hundred yards in front of me but my shell hole was deep enough so the close fire wouldn't bother much. They kept firing on that line, pouring in such a heavy concentration that the Jerries couldn't get through. One tank stuck its nose through the smoke and then exploded. It was the only one to get that far. I only saw three Jerry infantrymen on this side of the smoke. They came stumbling along, sort of dazed and I went after them with my carbine. They were so close I couldn't have missed if I had tried. It was like shooting fish in a barrel.

"The rest of them turned tail. The artillery upped the range and kept upping it and the doughboys came back to join in with their machine guns and then the whole doughboy outfit started ahead again. They chased the Jerries straight through their positions and kept on chasing them. That was all there was to it."

"Yes," Kennard said dryly. "He's still wondering why they gave him that Silver Star when all he did was talk on the radio a little."

# XV

ASIDE FROM Jack's great work (Kennard continued), the best thing about that day was that none of the casualties was serious. The worst was Sumner's broken arm. The report on Renburg was that he would be ready for duty again in about three weeks. When Venner came to, he had a bad headache which stayed with him for a couple of days but he was back on the job next morning, still batting for me, but in another twenty-four hours I was okay again, too. My arm still was a little stiff but it was my left one, so it didn't interfere with work.

Barrett was trying to figure whom he could spare to handle the radio for us when Barney Johns came back from the hospital, looking as if he had been on a vacation, so that problem was solved in the best possible way. Meanwhile Barrett had sent up another telephone man, named Gorning, a replacement who had just come to the battery. I was beginning to develop an obsession about wiremen about then and was glad I hadn't had to ask for him myself.

I needn't have worried. This Gorning is part horseshoe. He's tall and rangy, never seems to have a worry in the world and is always whistling. Whenever the telephone line went out, no matter how heavy the shellfire was, he'd just grab his tools and start out, whistling, and, in a little while, he'd be back, still whistling, without a scratch on him. I don't think the enemy shell or bullet ever will be made which will hit him. The next FO job I'm on, I'm going to requisition him if I have to take it all the way to General Marshall. He's the indestructible telephone man. We didn't lose him until the last week in April when we were headed for Bizerte. No, he wasn't wounded. He came down with the measles.

In the fighting, things were looking up for us. The battles were tough but we were winning all of them—El Guettar, Maknassy and the passes through the mountains. Of course, there had to be that American boner at Fondouk when we muffed the time schedule on a supposedly co-ordinated attack with the British and they finally had to do our part of the job. But that was the last time the Americans had to feel humiliated.

It was all hearsay to us in the FO detail. We were too busy attending to our own affairs but we gradually became conscious that we were getting the edge on the Jerries in every department. More troops and equipment kept pouring in and our air force became so strong we practically owned the sky. We didn't cut Rommel off as we had hoped but when we connected with the French and Montgomery's British Eighth army, all the Axis troops in Africa had been squeezed into one small corner of Tunisia. But there were a lot of them and they had a lot of equipment and it looked as if we still had a long hard job ahead before we squashed them.

Then General Eisenhower pulled his rabbit out of the hat. He made the gaudiest kind of preparations for a tremendous attack from the south with Montgomery's army carrying the mail. Von Arnim and Rommel—or maybe Rommel already was in Berlin, holding Hitler's head or vice versa—fell for it and weakened other sectors to mass troops and matériel down there to meet the expected drive. And then came the orders. The Second Corps was to swing up to the north and head for Bizerte and part of the British Eighth was sent to join General Anderson's British First for the drive on Tunis.

We never had moved so fast and, on our way, we did something else which was supposed to be as impossible, tactically, in this war as the tremendous feint General Eisenhower had pulled. The Second Corps cut directly through the British First Army, practically at right angles, and did it without confusion or delay.

Only a real army could have done it but, by that time, we were pretty close to being a real army and we knew it. We weren't cocky about ourselves now—just sure. And before Von Arnim had time even to wonder whether maybe he had put his eggs in the wrong basket, we were smashing our way toward Mateur and Anderson was going hellbent for Tunis.

It was no pushover but we knew what we were doing and how to do it and we knew we weren't going to be stopped this time. The infantry and the artillery were clicking like a machine and the air forces were working with the ground forces better than at any time. In our own small forward observation world, we finally were trying out the system of having the FO assigned to one doughboy outfit instead of to a zone and that worked better than anything we had used before.

The fighting was heavy all the time. Once more, we forgot what it meant to sleep. Then bad luck hit us again, the worst since Furman was killed. A doughboy runner, heading for us, was wounded about fifty yards from the observation post. Warren went out to help him. He had just about reached the doughboy when a burst of long range machine-gun fire caught him. Gorning saw it and made a dive out there. For about the first time, he wasn't whistling. Of course, nothing happened to *him*.

I had to stay where I was because the firing had revealed the position of the machine-gun nest and I called for fire on it. The hows came through in a hurry and we learned later every member of the machine-gun crews had been killed or seriously wounded.

That was the only consolation we had. Jack was badly wounded. Four bullets had hit him. But he was still alive. When he was taken back, we had a little hope for him but not much. We all felt like hell but we had learned long ago that the war wouldn't wait on our emotions. It just made us a little more bitter. Even Barney had the look about him after that.

Barrett sent up another instrument corporal, Charley Dale, who was a good man but he wasn't Warren. We all missed Jack like the devil, I especially. He was the only man in the detail who had been up there every day we had been in combat and I had leaned on him pretty heavily. Of all the original gang, only Barney and I were left, including the relief officers. Rick and Furman had been killed and Dolan and now Jack were in the hospital. The only sentiment we had left about the war was double-barreled hate.

Well, the last week in April, we crashed through the key hills where the Jerries had made their first strong stand and headed for the next one. It was about then that Gorning broke out with the measles. For a couple of days afterward, we all were worried and kept looking ourselves over for those red spots but, as usual, Gorning had done a solo job.

Then we pushed ahead to the last strong enemy line of defense of which Hill 509 was the key and the fighting stepped up to the hottest pitch yet. The Jerries were battling desperately because they knew if we broke through here, it was downhill all the way from Mateur to Bizerte and that meant curtains for them.

Bad luck hit the detail again when Dale was wounded so badly we knew he couldn't live. He was taken back but he died before they could get him on a hospital plane. The rest of the battery had suffered casualties, too, and Barrett told us he was so shorthanded he wouldn't be able to send us another corporal for a few days.

On our end of the line, the going was as tough as it was at the Hill. More men and guns came up but still we only seemed to inch ahead. Boyden, the telephone man who had replaced Gorning, was wounded and we couldn't get a new man for his spot either. So it was just Barney and myself up there. He kept the telephone line open while I handled the radio though, naturally, he had to be on the set when I was using the remote control. Then came the word that the big effort to break through was coming the next day.

We had one of the most advanced observation posts we ever had used and, from our foxholes, it looked as if the attack would be a tough and costly business in our zone unless we could smash practically every Jerry position with artillery before the doughboys had to tackle it. The trouble was, the Jerries were so good at concealment, it was tough locating the positions and we couldn't spot them all even from where we were.

I don't know when it struck me there *was* a way to spot them with certainty. A man behind the Jerry lines could do it and the way the front was, I felt sure one man could sneak through and find a hide-out from which he could radio fire missions long enough to do the necessary damage. A month or two before, I would have thought such a stunt was insane if I had thought of it at all but this was a month or two later in the pattern. Now, I not only was sure it could be done but that it had to be done.

I crawled up as far as I could go and located a gap where I thought it would be possible to get through after dark. I looked over the enemy territory a long time and finally spotted a place which looked good, about fifteen hundred yards behind the forward defense zone. It was a small rise, covered with brush. It was too low to be used by the Jerries for observation on our positions and too small to be used for anything else but it would be perfect for my purpose. Most important, there didn't seem to be anyone or anything alive near it. One of the reasons for that was the wide gap between the Nazi infantry and artillery. All through the campaign, the Jerries usually planted all their field pieces away back, a good deal farther behind their leading elements than we did on our side.

Barrett and Byrnes got together with me early in the evening and they finally okayed the idea. According to our final arrangement, I was to turn on the radio just once and just long enough to say "Kennard" after I was located. Then Barrett was to line up all the artillery he could. Once I started, in order to cut down the use of the radio and prevent its being located as long as possible and at the same time report the maximum number of targets, they were to be given in series of three or four and each mission was to be given in only four words, such as "Left three, over five. Left six, over two. Right four, short three." Each of these would be a separate fire mission, the numbers meaning hundreds of yards and the other words the reference to the base point. All necessary adjustment direction was to be in a maximum of four words in the same way. Target identification was to be given only when necessary to indicate whether the lights, mediums or heavies should take it.

While we were talking, the Jerry artillery interrupted us occasionally, with what effect we didn't know until, when we had about finished the details, Byrnes had a telephone call. All we heard him say was, "Yes, sir" but when he turned back to us, even in the dark we could see an odd expression on his face.

He said, "Major Barlow has just been wounded. I've been ordered back to the CP to take over the battalion. I'll have our end of it ready when you're under way."

You don't congratulate a man on a boost which comes over the body of another man, especially someone like Major Barlow. So we just shook hands with him. He turned the company over to his senior first, then he and Barrett started back and I went to break the news to Barney. He raised the roof when he found he wasn't included in the party.

"What would I be doing all by myself over here?" he said. "It would be just like sitting in the bleachers and watching the game when you're a member of one of the teams that's playing. It's going to be awfully tough for just one man to drag those radio cases alone. You might drop one or bang it against something and make a noise and then how long would you last? Besides, if you go alone, you'll have to stay in one place. With me along, you can use the remote control and observe more." I never heard words pour out of anyone so fast. Then, being Barney, he added, "But you are my superior officer and if you insist on winning the war by yourself, I can't stop you but you'll be sorry—sir."

Barney has a way with him. Besides, he made considerable sense. I thought I'd just save time and give in immediately. He started to pack the radio but I told him there was no hurry, we weren't going until midnight. That gave him time to do a lot of thinking and he came up with, "Sir, wouldn't it be a lot better if we had a telephone, too?"

I told him it would but it was impossible, if for no other reason than that we'd have to pack about twenty-five hundred yards of wire and the telephone instrument as well as the radio. Also, it would take too much time to lay it and wouldn't it be bright to notify the enemy exactly where we were by having an exposed line right to our door? He had all the answers again.

He said, "It's dollars to doughnuts they would think it was one of their own lines and anyway, I'll bury the last couple of hundred yards if we get located in time. I can fix it about the load, too. I'll get Ray Phillips, one of the doughboy telephone men to help until we start through the Jerries and I can handle the rest of it."

I said, "Then I suppose I take on both radio cases as I planned in the first place."

Without batting an eye, he answered, "Yes, sir, unless you'd rather run the wire, sir."

I asked him how about all the safety arguments he had used on me in the first place about the radio which made it so important for him to go along.

He said, "Well, you see, sir, our strategy has opened up a

little since then and I'm willing to have you take a little extra chance on the way up for the sake of safety when we get there."

I told him it was my hunch the only real reason he wanted to try to put through a telephone was because he thought it would be a swell gag on Hitler and Mussolini.

He just said, "Is there somebody named Mussolini?"

Even if it seemed insane, the idea of a telephone instead of the radio exclusively was alluring. If we could get away with it, it not only would make our job safer but our communications would be more certain as long as the telephone line stood up. Even if it were no more than half an hour, we might be able to do so much damage that the radio would be reasonably safe after that because of the confusion we hoped to cause among the Jerries.

I weakened but I asked him what gave him the idea a doughboy telephone man would stick out his neck unnecessarily—and probably in violation of orders—like that. Barney just looked at me wide-eyed. "Why, sir," he said, "he's one of my dearest pals." The real reason could happen only in the American Army.

Johns was laughing in his wheel chair. "It was my sister," he said. "Phillips and I had become very friendly and one day I showed him my sister's picture. I never saw anybody go overboard as fast as Phillips did. She's not bad but I didn't know she was that good. He kept after me to introduce him by mail and give him her address so he could write to her. I thought it was funny so, as a gag, I kept stalling him and every time I'd let him see her picture, he was worse. This night it paid off. I told him I couldn't very well recommend anybody to my sister who wasn't willing to take a little chance to help her brother. I told him if he did, I'd write to her the next day. Then I put the picture in my pocket and told him I would give it to him to use as a pin-up when he left us that night and that he'd find the address on the back of it. I wrote it while he was watching but not so he could see it. You know how sentimental doughboys get. After that, I owned him body and soul. I made good, too. My sister's writing to him regularly. And he's okay. She could do a lot worse."

# XVI

THINGS BECAME so quiet we started before midnight (Kennard resumed). All the excitement was in our minds. Actually, it was dull and tiresome. As an added precaution, we blackened our faces commando style and headed straight for the gap in the Jerry front. We were moving single file, about ten yards apart, Barney and I each carrying a radio case with Phillips lugging all the wire and the telephone and running the line at the same time as he crawled along. We spotted only one patrol and we never will know to which side it belonged because it was making as little noise as we were and it passed about twenty yards to our left.

When we started through the gap, the enemy positions on both sides of us were absolutely silent. Barney and I waited for Phillips to catch up with us and then we had troubles. He wanted to keep going. When I told him there wasn't a chance, he kept edging forward and I'd have to chase him down because we couldn't speak above a whisper. If he ever meets that sister of Barney's she's going to have a hard time getting away from him—if she wants to. I finally had to make it a positive order to him to go back and told him to stop endangering the life of his future brother-in-law.

When he was gone, Barney and I separated again, he taking over the telephone line. As I was carrying both radio cases, he didn't have much trouble keeping pace with me. But going through the enemy positions was about as dramatic as reading the telephone directory. Absolutely nothing happened, then, or after we were well inside the Jerry lines.

We slowed down a little to make it easier to watch our step because there were plenty of Jerries not too far away but our luck held until we were within thirty yards of the rise we were headed for and then we had a shock. There had been no Jerries around that position when I looked it over during the afternoon but there were some there now and, judging from the noise they were making with their shovels and their grumbling gutturals, they had just arrived. At that moment, I blessed Phillips for having delayed us, otherwise Barney and I might have been on that rise when the Jerries came.

The worst factor was the indication that the enemy was moving around in an area where he hadn't been before. I crawled away until I was well out of earshot of the group on the rise, waited for Barney, told him what was up and that he'd better stick close to me while we looked for a new spot.

Luck turned our way again. We ran into no more of the enemy and about ten minutes later we found what we were hunting, something like an overgrown mound, too small to be called a hill, apparently useless except to us, and it was covered with heavy brush.

We picked a spot for the radio where the bushes were particularly thick, listened until we were sure no one was near us, then began digging as rapidly and noiselessly as possible, spreading the dirt we unearthed under the bushes, hoping we were doing it well enough so it wouldn't be detected by daylight. When we were pretty well along with that, I crawled to a slightly higher spot which had the same heavy undergrowth and began digging my own foxhole, one of the bottle shaped kind into which I could slide down if necessary.

Before I was finished, Barney came over with the remote control, then went back to the set and I made my one word broadcast. In less than five seconds, I heard the "Right" which meant I had been heard and we switched off.

Barney slipped off into the dark to bring in the telephone and I went on digging. We had worked at night so much that by now we could see fairly well with nothing more than starlight to help. I looked around to orient myself, then crouched down in the foxhole, shaded the opening and studied my map by flashlight. The most pleasant realization was that our position was almost directly on the gun-target line from the battery position to the base point, which would make calculations much easier. The base point itself was about five hundred yards beyond us toward the enemy rear. It looked as if we were lucky to have missed out on our first choice of positions.

Barney wriggled up with the telephone about two hours later. He said he had buried the wire as he came along and it was underground most of the last two hundred yards to our mound, except for short stretches where it practically hid itself under the brush. He gave me some slack, clipped on the instrument, then slipped away again to bury the last stretch of wire up the slope to the foxhole.

I crawled down into the foxhole again to cover my voice, then called the battery for a check. I hadn't more than identified myself to the battery operator when Barrett was on the line. He said, "I thought you'd be behind 'em by now." When I told him I was, he asked, "With a telephone?" I said "Yes" and he came back, "My God!" I said, "I'll be calling" and shut off.

Just in time, too, Barney barely had finished covering the line into the foxhole when we both heard the tramp of feet behind us. We just flattened out and held our breath.

A considerable body of Jerries was coming and we thought they would climb right over us but, at the last moment, they veered and went around the hump. After they had passed, Barney was starting for his own dugout when we heard some more boots. These went around the other side of us and faded toward the forward positions. Barney made a quick crawl to his own hole and then we heard still more troops in motion. For the next hour, they were moving up, all headed forward, but none of them stopped anywhere near us. But that they were massing for a strong stand was certain.

Then, at last, the sky began to turn gray and a few minutes later, I could see that this was a good place. From here, we could see everything the Jerries had on this sector. I verified that we were on the base point gun-target line and, as it grew a little brighter, saw that the Jerries had brought up just about everything they had during the night. There were so many targets in sight, I hardly knew where to begin. I made some quick calculations on those that seemed the most important, then dropped down into my foxhole and called Barrett.

"Ready?" I said.

"With lots of artillery," he answered, "and the doughboys are set to go."

"Okay," I said, "let's go." I gave him four missions, then straightened up to observe results. For about thirty seconds there was absolute quiet. Then there was a regular hurricane of blasts and hell came down on the Jerries.

After that it was wild, the wildest experience I've ever known. As we had expected, when daylight came on, adjustment of fire became practically unnecessary. The shells were smashing in on their targets on the first round time after time. I was pattering out missions and adjusting fire as fast as I could pour out the words, only worried that I might get things mixed up between the lights, mediums and heavies but my luck stayed with me. It was no credit to me. That was the softest job of fire direction I ever had. Anybody who knew that three feet make a yard could have done it.

Our guns just ripped up and down the sector, smashing target after target, crashing into the middle of troop concentrations and making an inferno of the whole area. When the Jerries opened up with their artillery, the batteries signed their own death warrants because that made it easy to spot them and our mediums and heavies did the rest.

I lost all sense of time so I don't know how long we had been giving them that kind of fire when the confusion started. The Jerries didn't know where to turn. Their positions were being blown to pieces. When they tried to leave them, they ran into a hail of steel and TNT in the open. When they tried to burrow into their holes, our time fire got a lot of them and discouraged the rest. Their officers charged around, barking orders, trying to get the men back into some kind of order but they weren't having much luck.

Then all along the advanced zone, machine gun, rifle and mortar fire became terrific. I wondered what had been wrong with our fire on those positions until I saw Jerries begin to pour back from there and realized it was our own doughboys who were doing the shooting.

I tried to call for fire on the retreating Heinies and discovered the telephone had gone out at last but, by that time, it had served us mighty well and more than vindicated Barney for suggesting it.

I dropped the telephone instrument into the foxhole and picked up the remote control. I wasn't worried about its being detected now. No Jerry in this neighborhood was interested in anything except saving his own life.

Away up ahead, I could see our doughboys coming into sight, now. Then I heard a lot of racket behind us and turned to see the Jerries bringing up field pieces—eighty-eights and one-o-fives—rushing them into position for point-blank fire. They swung out on both sides of our mound and it looked as if we were going to be in the middle of the line but they were far enough away on both sides so they couldn't hear or see us yet.

I called for fire on them and told Barney to keep his head down because, while we were a little above the guns and not too near them, any stray shell of ours could annoy us. In fact, it wouldn't even have to be a stray and I began to get some idea of how Rick must have felt that last day.

The Jerries had just loaded their guns when a curious thing happened. It sounded as if two of our shells hit with only a split second difference between them beside one of the eighty-eights. The gun seemed to sail straight up into the air and then it exploded. I heard the chunks of metal sizzling past my head and one of them sliced off some of the bushes in front of me. The gun crew had been wiped out.

I tried to call in another mission but nothing happened. I climbed out of my foxhole and wriggled over to Barney's dugout. Barney was stretched out on his back, unconscious and for a second I thought he was dead, except that there was no sign of blood on him. The radio set was beside him—in pieces—a total wreck. One of the fragments of that exploded gun had blown in and smashed it. So our day's work was over. I leaned over Barney to find out what had knocked him out and saw a pretty fair sized bump rising on the side of his head so it looked as if he had taken a wallop from part of the radio set. I poured some water on the bump and his face from my canteen and he was just blinking his eyes and coming back to consciousness when I heard somebody yell, *"Schweinhund!"* behind me—to a Nazi, everybody is a *"schweinhund"* who isn't on his side—and I swung around to see a Jerry leveling his rifle at me.

I thought this was it, all right, but just as he was pulling the trigger, another Heinie jumped at him, yelled, *"Dumkopf!"* and gave him a sock on the jaw that sent him rolling and the shot went over my head. Barney had pulled himself into a sitting position and was shaking the fog out of his head when this second Jerry covered us with a pistol and barked, *"Haende auf!"* There wasn't much doubt as to what he meant, so our hands went up.

"This is a fine finish," Barney muttered. The Jerry waved his pistol at him and yelped, "Still!" and then, *"Kommen sie. Mach schnell,"* and he waved us out of the dugout.

We crawled out and tried to sneak a look toward the front to see whether there were any chance of our gang getting there in time to rescue us but the Jerry pushed us around and then, in practically perfect English said, "To the rear. Hurry. We want you alive. That fool would have shot you."

Barney said, "Thanks, pal," but after that we didn't have a chance to speak. We were given the Nazi version of the bum's rush and it was a good one. I don't know why we weren't knocked off by the fire from our own men because we were on our feet and practically running but they missed us and the next thing we knew, we were bundled into some kind of truck and were highballing toward the Nazi headquarters.

# XVII

THERE'S NO USE pretending Barney and I accepted the idea of being prisoners very cheerfully, particularly when we realized that if we hadn't been discovered for fifteen or twenty minutes more, our own troops would have been past us and we would have been safe. But here we were and there wasn't much we could do about it.

The Jerry who had captured us went along. He felt pretty good about his haul and he was in a conversational mood.

"You are Americans, of course," he said.

Barney said, "Yep, part of the bunch which is knocking hell out of you."

The Jerry scowled and said, "You are impertinent—and you will not see any of the knocking. You are part of that—that bunch—no longer. You are going to Germany."

"I joined the army so I could see the world," said Barney.

The Jerry said, "I am Lieutenant Brasch." He turned to me. "You are an officer, no doubt," he said.

"Both of us are officers," said Barney.

"You," said Lieutenant Brasch, "are lying. You are not an officer."

Barney just shrugged his shoulders and said, "Can a guy be shot for trying?"

"In the army of the Reich, he can," Lieutenant Brasch snapped.

Barney said, "Well, there you are. That's why I joined the American Army. We do it differently."

"And very badly," said Brasch, with a thin sort of smile.

Barney took a long look back toward the battle, then turned to Brasch and grinned. "Oh, I don't know," he said. "We're doing all right."

Brasch went red and raised his hand as if he were going to slap Barney across the face, then seemed to think better of it. "You talk too much," he said. "You will keep quiet."

"Okay," said Barney, "I'm getting a little bored anyway."

Brasch turned to me. "I would treat him as he deserves," he said, his voice sore, "but the Herr Oberst wants his prisoners able to talk when he interviews them—before sending them on their way to Germany."

I thanked him and he took me seriously. He said it was quite all right. I asked him where he had learned his English and for the first time, he laughed.

"I went to school in your country," he said. "I was graduated from a university there in 1937."

I said, "I suppose you agented for der Fuehrer on the side."

Brasch gave me that knowing, contemptuous smile at which the Nazis are so good. "Of course," he said. "That was the big reason I was there. I sent home much valuable information."

I lost interest in talking to him after that and the conversation lagged. Finally, we reached a headquarters where we were taken out of the truck and into the presence of a Nazi colonel, one of the beer-barrel kind who looked something like Bismarck. He could speak perfect English, too. Efficient folks, the Nazis. The Colonel seemed a little jittery, though. He dismissed Brasch immediately and said he would take us on one at a time. He decided to quiz Barney first, probably on the mistaken theory that an American enlisted man will give up information more readily than an officer. As a matter of fact, a prisoner of war can be required to tell no more than his name, rank and serial number. Our orders from Allied Headquarters were to decline to answer any other questions in case of capture. But everybody always tries to learn more than that from prisoners, of course. As Barney went into the Colonel's room, he gave me a heavy wink. I had a hunch he was going to show willingness to answer any and all questions

—in his own way. Barney's imagination is very good in an emergency.

He hadn't been in that other room more than two minutes before I could hear the Colonel shouting at the top of his lungs in a mixture of German and English and there wasn't any doubt his goat was being led around on a string by Barney. Then the door flew open and a guard came rushing toward me, ordering me inside immediately.

The Colonel was standing behind his desk, his face like a red thundercloud. Barney stood opposite him with the expression of an innocent lamb, looking as if he were hurt by the Colonel's rage. When he looked around at me, he said, "Gosh, I'm glad you're here, Lieutenant. The Colonel is being mean to me."

God knows our situation wasn't exactly the best in the world but it was tough keeping a straight face on that one. The Colonel roared, "Silence!" at Barney, then turned to me and shouted, "This *schweinhund* tells me nothing but lies. Nobody lies to me. I do not permit. I will ask you the same questions. If your answers are not the same, I will order him taken out and shot."

Barney suddenly became belligerent. He leaned across the desk and said, "Now, look here, Colonel, or *oberst*, or whatever you are, I'm a qualified prisoner of war, entitled to all the rights and privileges guaranteed by the Geneva Convention and if you think——"

That was as far as he got. The Colonel yelled, "Quiet!" He looked at Barney as if he would like to tear him apart on the spot but finally swung toward me and barked, "What is your name?"

I said, "James Kennard, first lieutenant," and added my serial number.

The Colonel asked, "What is your organization? What is your branch of service?"

I said, "I must respectfully decline to answer, sir."

The Colonel's face worked like an accordion for a minute, then he yelped, "You what? Why?"

For some reason or other, I just couldn't resist pitching one. I said, "I decline to answer on the grounds that what I say may incriminate, degrade and endanger me and a fellow soldier."

Barney said, "Hot dog!" but the Colonel looked as if he were going to burst a blood vessel. He sputtered and pawed the air and I think he was just going to order us both shot when there was a loud knock on the door.

The Colonel made a stab at collecting himself and called, "*Herein.*" A young officer came in, saluted and pattered out German faster than I could follow it but one thing was certain—what he was saying wasn't good. The Colonel seemed to sag. For a minute, as he looked at us, he wasn't seeing us at all. Then he came to and yelled, "*Heraus!* Get out! You are not important now. Get out!" He snapped a couple of commands to the guards and we were marched away. He was barking to the young officer at top speed as we left.

As we were hustled along, Barney said, "What do you think, sir?" I said it was my hunch the Colonel had been told our army had crashed through and maybe his headquarters wouldn't be healthy very long. That had been the drift of the few words I had understood.

We were rushed into another truck and headed north. None of our guards spoke English and they refused to allow us to speak to each other. They were quiet themselves, too, so there was no chance to figure what was what.

It was late afternoon when we finally rolled into a town on a landlocked harbor and realized we had reached Bizerte. The idea left us a little sour. We had expected to get here but not this way.

We were driven to an old stone building, half-ruined by bombs and were dumped out of the truck. The place was doing emergency service as a hole for prisoners of war. We saw half a dozen other Americans in it but the silence order still was in effect and we didn't have a chance to talk with them.

Barney and I were pitched into the same dark room. This puzzled us at first until it dawned upon us the place undoubtedly was rigged up so somebody could listen in on anything we said. If that was the idea, any report of our conversation must have given somebody a headache trying to figure it out.

The room itself was a filthy hole with no beds except a couple of heaps of straw, crawling with millions of every kind of bug known to Africa. The Jerries hadn't taken our cigarettes and matches so we were consoling ourselves with a smoke when a guard called us out and we were lined up for what passes for prisoner chow among the Heinies.

We were given a small helping of some kind of foul stew, a hunk of dry, black bread and lukewarm water. We managed to eat some of it because we were hungry. We hadn't had any food since daylight.

While we were at it, a Nazi officer came over to me and said, in the same good English the others had used, "You are Lieutenant Kennard?" When I admitted it, he said, "As an officer, you will be given better quarters and food but not tonight. We have more important matters at hand than mere prisoners."

"So it's going as badly as that?" I said.

He snapped, "Everything goes according to plan," and turned his back on us while Barney yelled after him, "You tell 'em—*our* plan."

When we were back in our cell, we didn't know what to do about sleeping. The straw was out of the question, so much so that Barney finally said, "Let's see if this starts anything" and struck a match to it after heaping it in one corner with his foot.

It was a nice blaze and since the walls were stone and there was nothing in the room except the straw, the bugs and ourselves, it couldn't do much damage. But it certainly brought action. Guards came running into the cell and dragged us out, yelling, *"Schweinhunde"* in their best manner. We were hauled before the officer who had spoken to us before. He swore at us in German for a while and when Barney carefully explained he had set the fire by accident when the match slipped from his fingers while he was looking under the bed for burglars, the Jerry ordered our cigarettes and matches taken away. I became sore and protested and he finally made a typical Nazi compromise. Because I was an officer, he gave me back my cigarettes and matches but kept Barney's and then ordered us back to the same cell we had had, probably thinking he was punishing us by depriving us of that bug-infested straw. Barney said he considered it a clear-cut victory and promptly borrowed a cigarette and light from me.

The fire had killed off a lot of the bugs, leaving only four or five million still alive, so we evolved a system of sleeping standing up, leaning against each other in a corner. It worked after a fashion. At least, we dozed most of the night, awakened once in a while by the roar of the guns on the front.

The next morning, we were lined up for more bad food, then were sent back to our cells. What little I could make of the guards' conversation, the Jerries were plenty worried about what would happen in the next couple of days.

We were left in our cells all day, except for the meals. Nobody came near us or called us up for questioning, so we knew there still was no time for "mere prisoners." But there was plenty of excitement. All day, squadrons of bombers came over and dropped their eggs. The roar of the explosions was with us all the time, although the bombs seemed to be falling only along the water front and none struck near us.

The next day was May 6 and it started just like the day before. No move was made to give me new quarters, which was okay as I didn't want to be separated from Barney. But, shortly after noon, we were hauled out and taken to the Nazi intelligence headquarters. Just to make these quizzes easier on ourselves and to get some kick out of the situation, we had decided to answer questions. We had cooked up a line in which we both were letter-perfect so our stories would jibe and we only hoped the Jerries would believe what we told them and act upon it.

It didn't take long to grasp that this intelligence officer had a good deal more on the ball than our friend the Colonel. He took us one at a time—Barney first again—asked his questions smoothly, never seemed to doubt our word and made notes of all our answers. He was a lean, hard-faced, fishy-eyed animal and seemed to enjoy taking a lot of time about the whole business. It was fairly late by the time he had finished with me. Then he called Barney back, gave us both an icicle smile and said, "You understand, of course, I know everything you have told me is false. We are not as stupid as you think—perhaps not even as stupid as Americans."

He gave us another of those unfunny smiles as he looked at his notes, and said, "What you two have told me agrees so perfectly, I could almost think it had been rehearsed. So, perhaps it was. Well, we will give you time for more rehearsals on your way to Italy, where you will be questioned again. After that, you will have one more chance—when you reach Germany. Let me advise you to tell the truth when you are questioned in Germany. Things are much more pleasant for those who do not try to deceive the Fuehrer."

Then he bowed us out as if we were guests of honor. At the door he said, "You now will be taken aboard ship for your trip to Naples. When it will sail depends upon your bombers. It is a little unpleasant, waiting in the harbor. I do hope you are not killed your own fliers."

This time he did send us on our way and, sure enough, we were marched down to the harbor and rowed out to an Italian coastal steamer which was serving as a transport. It was anchored well out from shore. Our bombers hadn't left Bizerte enough docks to flag a handcar.

We were crammed into a sort of oversized cage with some forty or fifty other American and British prisoners, below decks. It was hot down there but not as dirty as our cell on shore. There were no bunks, just some benches, because the run to Italy was short.

Just when we were beginning to think it was a lot better than our cell, another wave of our bombers came over and hell poured down all around us. We began to appreciate what the intelligence officer had meant but, apparently, our airmen weren't aiming for our transport that time and we escaped damage.

There was a good deal of commotion all over the ship and one of the Britishers who understood Italian said he heard a sailor who passed our cage say we were going to pull out after dark. Our gloom over the news was becoming as thick as fog when we began hearing more explosions, which spelled another raid.

The bursts were much nearer this time and finally came one which almost deafened us and the ship gave a lurch that made us sure it had been hit. Then the bombing stopped. We could hear a lot of shouting in Italian and a little later, our Italian-speaking Britisher hailed another sailor who told him the bomb had damaged the ship just enough so it would not be able to leave that night, but repairs would be made so we could leave with a convoy in the morning.

We stretched out wherever we could find room and grabbed what sleep we could. In the morning, after some more unspeakable food, our interpreter learned the ship was ready to go and all the crew were on edge to get under way before our bombers started coming over on the milk run. Finally, the engines began to throb and we felt the ship moving. We were on our way to a German prison camp.

# XVIII

WE ALL FELT pretty low. We hadn't said much about it but there wasn't one of us in that cage who hadn't hoped and more or less believed some miracle would happen and that our army would capture Bizerte before the convoy could pull out. Now that long chance had faded.

I guess the captain of the transport figured there wasn't much danger of our starting anything so, after we had been under way for a while, some guards came down and unlocked the cage and waved us toward the deck, telling our British interpreter we could take the air for a couple of hours but would have to stay in formation.

When we reached topside, we were passing the headlands above Bizerte and heading for the open sea. The sun felt good and it was a pleasure to inhale the fresh air. There were eight or ten ships in the convoy, most of them about like the one we were on, all of them apparently going full speed.

The crew of our transport seemed to spend most of its time looking back toward Bizerte, eyes aloft and worried. We took on the habit, except that we were anxious instead of worried. I don't know just how long we had been at it when we saw the specks in the sky, so far away we weren't sure they meant anything. Then one of the Italian sailors let out a yell and pointed at them. In a second, everybody in the crew was jabbering and waving his arms. Then the skipper squealed a couple of orders from the bridge and the gun crews started on the run for their battle stations.

The specks in the sky were growing both in size and numbers and they began to look a lot like Fortresses and Liberators and Lightnings.

The ship veered sharply to starboard and began to zigzag

away from the rest of the convoy which was trying its best to scatter. But it needed more time than they had with troubles coming at better than three hundred miles an hour. Almost before our ship was away on its first tack we heard that whistling scream which only a P-38 makes in a dive. I don't think it occurred to any of us just then that we were in as much danger as the crew of the ship. All we did when that twin-tailed Lightning came swooping down on us was wave and yell at the top of our voices. I guess all that saved us was the sharp change in direction the ship was given as the plane dropped its two eggs. One of them fell a good hundred and fifty yards away. The other was nearer, near enough so the ship gave a heave which almost knocked us off our feet. The anti-aircraft guns were peppering away at the Lightning but apparently did not even come close because the plane simply zoomed up and began circling to come back for some strafing.

Then it suddenly seemed as if the whole sky were full of our planes, the fighters and the heavy and medium bombers, winging down on the whole convoy. The air was just a solid roar of flak and exploding bombs and machine-gun fire from the planes. Over to the west, we heard a terrific explosion, followed by several others in quick succession and we saw one of the convoy ships wrapped in a blinding sheet of flame. Then the glare died and the ship simply broke in two with each end burning as it sank. Farther over, another ship was burning with the smoke rolling high.

It was about that time the captain of our transport awoke to the fact that all his prisoners were on deck and he ordered us rushed below. Our protests didn't help us. The guards came at us with bayonets and we were hustled down to our cage.

The noise overhead was terrific and the ship was bobbing around like a cork as the skipper tried to wriggle it through that barrage of bombs. How we escaped a direct hit is beyond

me. Even the big four-motored planes were flying exceptionally low before they dropped their loads. Some of them
fell close enough so the ship would stagger as if it were
drunk and we expected the sides to cave in any second but it
still bobbed and weaved around while the roar of the explosions kept on.

Sailors were running back and forth past our cage constantly, always yelling excitedly at each other. Our interpreter kept listening. Suddenly, he seemed to be startled and
his face looked as if he didn't dare believe what he heard. We
began asking him what went on but he waved us to be quiet
and yelled a question at one of the passing sailors who barked
just, "*Si*," as he rushed on up to the top deck. The Britisher
swung toward us, grinning from ear to ear and he yelled,
"Bli'me, the ship's giving it up. We're headed back for
Bizerte. Thought that was what the blighters were saying."

We let out a roar at that, only hoping it was true, not car-
ing a damn that we stood a swell chance of being blown up
any minute on the way. Anything seemed better than going
on to a Nazi concentration camp.

The hellish racket above us went on and on. It seemed
endless and all of us began to be half seasick from the ship's
constant change of pace and direction. Whatever else may
have been the matter with him, that Italian skipper knew
how to juggle his ship under an air attack.

Then the bomb bursts suddenly stopped and anti-aircraft
fire died away, so we knew the raid was over. We wondered
if the skipper would change his mind now and try for
Naples again. Our British pal hailed a passing sailor—they
still seemed to be hopping around like fleas—and stopped
him long enough to learn that seven ships of the convoy had
been sunk or set afire and there wasn't a chance in the world
of our skipper's trying to make Italy practically alone.

We whooped it up again—a little too soon. Just a couple
of minutes later, all the anti-aircraft guns were blazing away

again and once more came the crash of exploding bombs. Barney looked at me and said, "Something tells me the skipper's luck has just about run out. From here on the percentage is all against him."

He barely had the words out of his mouth when we heard a terrific explosion which made us all stone deaf for a few seconds. The ship seemed to jump out of the water, then settle back with a kind of quiver which wasn't so good. We heard a lot of wild yelling and the ship pitched and rolled as if it were on another drunk. Not one of us doubted the transport was going to sink. We began beating against the cage and yelling to be released and given a chance to get on deck at least.

If the skipper had been a Nazi, I'm dead certain we would have been left where we were but, even if they have strayed pretty far in the wrong direction, most Italians have a heart and a sense of decency. This skipper hadn't had time to hear about our howling to be set free so he undoubtedly thought of it on his own. Anyway, our guards came down, unlocked the cage and let us up on deck.

When we scrambled up to the open air, the sky was full of our planes again, circling around and apparently getting ready for the kill. That was probably the only time we ever hoped our bombers would miss their target. We already were so close to port it was tough to realize our chances of making it were so slim.

Forward the deck was a shambles with a huge hole in the deck itself. But this was only half the story. Barney leaned over the rail and pointed toward the bow. We all looked over and saw a gaping hole just above the water line.

Then the ship went into a funny maneuver. The skipper swung it completely around and, so help me, he started into the Bizerte harbor, stern first, running away from the hole in the bow so he wouldn't ship water.

Another bomb came down and we all fell on our faces

while it splashed into the water alongside and exploded. The transport gave another sickening lurch and then a sailor came running up from below decks, yelling something which the Britisher interpreted as a report that there was another hole in the side and the Mediterranean was pouring in.

We could see the skipper up on the bridge, shouting orders, trying desperately to keep his ship under way. Then another Fortress came swooping down. We saw the bomb bay open and the egg dropped out, straightened and then we heard that whistling sound a falling bomb makes. As we flopped again we knew it was going to be a direct hit. The explosion was so tremendous, we were completely stunned for a few seconds while the ship jumped and heaved and splinters of metal and wood showered in all directions. Three or four of our fellows were nicked by them.

When the fog cleared out of our heads and we looked up, we knew this was the finish. The bridge and all the superstructure around it was gone, completely wiped out—the skipper, too, of course—and the whole after part of the ship was on fire. We barely had time to notice that much when another explosion knocked us over. This hit was forward and all the twisted wreckage there began blazing, too.

There had been a lot of casualties. Dead and wounded members of the crew were all over what was left of the deck. When we jumped up and started for the lifeboats which was all there was left to do now, we discovered one of the British prisoners had been killed by the last bomb.

What happened after that wasn't pretty. A bunch of the sailors went into a panic. Some of the lifeboats had been damaged, naturally, but, with all the casualties, there still were plenty for everyone left alive. But these hysterical Italians went crazy and started clawing and beating their way over everybody else. Our guards were trying to keep some semblance of order and led us toward boats which could handle all of us easily when that screaming gang came charging at us, very obviously to trample us down and take our boats.

That called off all bets. We had been tired of inaction anyway and we just decided no panic-stricken sailor was going to be saved over our shining white bodies. We sailed into them, whaling away with both fists. It was a little one-sided because they were only scared while we were mad and knew what we wanted to do. The funny part of it was our guards stayed with us and helped. I don't know how many of them we knocked cold but we plowed through and climbed into the boats. When the hysterical ones tried to jump in and push us away, we either bopped them back on deck or pitched them into the ocean. We weren't particular. Two of our guards climbed into each of the boats and they kept their guns trained on the wild mob on deck while we lowered away. I don't know how many of those fear-crazy sailors got away. I do know everybody who kept his head escaped the burning ship. Boatloads full were coming down on both sides of it.

As soon as we hit the water, we started pulling the oars, hoping to God, now, that our fliers would be tired of shooting our way. Barney and I had stayed together through the whole mess and he was on an oar just across from me. When I looked over at him he was grinning. I asked him why and he said, "I was just thinking—this is the most advanced forward observation post we've ever had. I just never figured we'd ever have one in a rowboat." Then he said, "Now, if we just had a radio——"

"We'd ask those fellows upstairs to use something else for a target," I said.

Barney sobered and looked up and saw the planes circling over us. He said, "Wouldn't you think they'd have had enough by now? I don't think a single ship of that convoy is still floating."

I said, "Their orders are to kill and keep on killing until

there's no enemy left to knock off. We're just unlucky to be mixed with the wrong gang." I was feeling a little grim about it. The shore, only a couple of hundred yards away now, was so near and yet so far.

Just then, the planes dived for us. Their eggs and machine-gun fire sprayed all around us. One of the boats filled with Italian sailors vanished completely in the explosion of a direct hit. We saw men keel over in some of the other boats. In our own, one of our guards caught a machine-gun bullet through the shoulder.

We pulled those oars until it seemed as if our arms would drop off, trying to get to shore before any more planes came our way. But we were landlubbers and not very good at it. We were still a hundred yards from shore when our planes came down again. We tried waving at them but, of course, that did no good. One of them came shooting by, right over our heads. There was a heavy explosion and I was knocked loose from my oar. I heard the crash of splintering wood and then I saw the other side of the boat had been bashed in completely so that we were sinking and Barney was lying huddled in the water in the middle of the boat, his whole side a mass of blood.

All I had time to do was heave him up on my shoulder and tumble overside just as the boat turned turtle. It was heavy going, swimming with all my clothes on but it wasn't so far to shore now and I made it by trailing Barney behind me, doing my best to keep his head out of water.

The planes overhead were still strafing away. Their machine-gun bullets were whistling past us and their bombs were dropping everywhere. When I finally touched bottom and struggled on shore, I could see only two lifeboats still afloat, although a good many of the occupants of those which had been sunk were making it to shore.

I dragged Barney up above the water line and ripped away his shirt. The gash in his side looked bad and I went through my pockets trying to find something with which I could give him first aid. I could see another of the lifeboats nearing shore not far away when a bomb burst directly in front of it. I felt a numbing shock in my leg as I fell down but for a second I had the crazy idea it was just concussion.

I heard a lot of wild yells on the shore above me. When I looked up, I thought I was delirious because I was seeing American soldiers, a lot of American soldiers, charging down the slope toward us. All the Italians who had reached shore had their arms in the air. It came to me sort of vaguely that the air strafing had stopped. I tried to stand up but found I couldn't, so I raised my arms, too, but I waved them to let our soldiers know I was one of them not surrendering to them.

I tried to yell. Maybe I did. I don't know. A terrific pain shot through my leg. I looked down and saw I was blood from hip to ankle and there was blood on my chest and arms. I began to feel dizzy. All I could think was that, somehow, the nightmare of being a prisoner was over and we were back with our own gang. I tried to yell and wave at them again. For a second there seemed to be a lot of them all around me. Then the lights went out.

# XIX

WHEN I CAME TO, I first was conscious of a roaring sound I thought must be in my head. A swaying motion went with it and I couldn't account for that. I heard another sound, somebody groaning, then realized I was the groaner myself. A nurse came from somewhere and I heard myself croaking something about where was I. She said I was on an ambulance plane and I must not try to talk. The order was superfluous. Almost before she had said it, I was out again.

The next time I came out of the fog, I was in a bed, there was no motion and no engine roar, so I thought the plane must have landed. I shut my eyes to think but that was too much so I opened them again and tried looking around—which wasn't much easier. I could see a couple of nurses and a man in a white uniform not far from my bed. They seemed to be talking but I couldn't hear anything they said. I thought I could see other beds, too. It slowly began to add up and I came to a brilliant conclusion—I was in a hospital.

One of the nurses happened to look my way and saw my eyes were open. She came toward me, smiling. I've never been able to figure out what difference it makes where you are when you can't do anything about it anyway but that's always the first thing anyone asks when they come to after being out for a while and I'm no different from anyone else. So I asked the nurse just that. My voice was so weak I could barely hear it myself and she, too, told me not to try to talk. She told me I was in a base hospital at Algiers.

She was still smiling. So were the other nurse and the doctor. All this good cheer in a hospital didn't seem right to me and, orders or no orders, I asked why everybody was so happy. She said why shouldn't they be? The last of the enemy troops in Africa had surrendered. The campaign was over. We had taken a couple of hundred thousand prisoners.

That didn't add up right. All that couldn't have happened since yesterday and just yesterday we had captured Bizerte. There hadn't been time to mop up all the loose Jerries and Italians. So I thought she was kidding. But I didn't care much about the whole thing. Something about the name "Algiers" seemed a lot more important but I couldn't figure what. I was still trying to think about it when I went back into the fog.

Maybe your mind dopes out the answers to things while you're asleep. Anyway, the next time I awoke, the first thing that came to me was that I knew all about the significance of Algiers. It had meant Betty and Rick and the three of us together, snatching a few perfect hours in the middle of war. Now it still meant Betty Ware—Betty Ware and a special kind of torture. I just lay there with my eyes shut, wishing for a minute I hadn't come out of the fog at all.

Then I became conscious of another sound near me, an odd sound I couldn't quite make out. Gradually it dawned upon me it was someone crying and trying to suppress any audible sobs. I began to realize the sound was right beside my bed. Maybe it was a warning flash but for some reason I didn't want to open my eyes. When I finally did, there was Betty.

I guess something of what flashed through my mind must have shown in my face because she cried, "Don't look like that," in a half-choked way. Then she stooped and kissed me and her head stayed down there beside mine. When she spoke again, I knew I was dreaming because she began to whisper things I never had expected to hear from her—that it was all she had been praying for, that I would come back to her alive, that I had been all wrong about her and Rick, there never had been a question of choice between us, I had been the one from the first.

I didn't want to wake up—and I haven't yet. I guess I never will.

After that, I gradually began to learn things, such as the fact that I had been out for a week and that there had been a lot of doubt about me until the day I finally awoke and saw Betty. Then I came up fast. Who wouldn't? I learned that she had been sitting at my bedside every night all night after working all day, ever since they had brought me there.

I learned I had been cut up quite a little and my left leg had been rather badly mangled, so they were going to ship me back to the United States by plane to recuperate. I had been delirious and had raved a good deal about Barney and Jack, so Betty had found out about them. Jack already had been sent home, still in a serious condition but with good hope of his recovery. Barney was badly hurt but would pull through and was scheduled to go back on the same plane with me.

When I told Betty how her letters had crossed me up, she laughed and said I wasn't very good at feminine psychology or I would have known she could write so freely to Rick because he never was more than a comrade but it was much harder to be just friendly in letters to someone for whom she really cared so, naturally, she leaned in the other direction.

When we talked about my plane trip home I told her I'd be back sooner than she expected and she said, "Of course, you will," a bit too quickly though I didn't get it at the time.

I asked her if she would marry me when I came back and she said, "No." That floored me and I guess I looked a little blank and stupid about it, so she laughed and said, "No, not when you come back. When you come back, I want to have been married to you ever since you left—or am I rushing you?" I told her I was in the mood for it and then she came right back with, "How about tomorrow?" It couldn't be too soon for me but I didn't think she meant it so I said, "Why not today?" She looked at me for a second, then said, "It's a deal," and that's how it happened. Two hours later, we were married, there in the hospital and I was off in the clouds until I began to do a little thinking. I *had* been rushed a little. There must be a reason.

The next time the doctor came around, I pinned him down and he told me. I was going to be lame, he said, and my soldiering days were over. It was quite a blow. I hadn't been suffering much pain, so when they had told me I was going to recover, I just took it for granted that I'd be all right. So, now, I just refused to believe him and that still goes. I asked him if Betty knew and he said, surprised, of course, she had known all along.

I felt very hollow inside and when my bride came to see me that night, I asked her if what I suspected was true about that marriage of ours. Some girls would have laughed it off. Betty didn't. She just said, "Yes, Jim. Please don't be sorry." I looked at her and said, "I never could be that," and knew I meant it.

She smiled then and said, "You see, I pretty much want to belong to you and I want you to belong to me and I was afraid you might not let that happen if you knew you weren't coming back."

I asked her, "Who says I'm not coming back? What makes *you* think I won't?"

She just sat there and looked at me, staring into my eyes for I don't know how long until something began to dawn in hers, something I liked. "The doctors tried to make me think it," she said, "but I've just changed my mind. You'll be back and you will be as good as new. I know it."

So that makes two of us who know it and, the way I feel about Betty, she and I make a majority any time. But the biggest thing she did for me was take away the black cloud which had hung over me ever since Rick was killed. She finally made me talk about it, the day before the plane left and she said something I'll never forget.

"It broke my heart when your letter came," she said, "because you and I had lost our best friend but I was more heartbroken about you. Rick was killed, yes, but you had to go on living and remembering. I hear they are going to give you a medal for what you did the day you were captured but I think the action for which you really should be decorated was giving those orders which meant Rick's death. That was so much harder to do—but it had to be done—so you did it. That's what Rick would have done. You owe it to him to see it that way."

Somehow that did it. I still have plenty of bad dreams. I guess you can't escape them when you've lived through the kind of things that Jack and Barney and I have. But we have to go back to them. The job isn't finished. It's only begun, and I've just learned how to do my part. I can't waste all that education. So I'll be back there. I have to be. There's a soldier over there waiting for me to come back "as good as new."

Anyway, I don't like it over here—not now—but I won't go into that. There's just one place I want to be, the place where I belong, where I'll be calling "Fire mission" again and watching our howitzers smashing something else that's in our way—until we've smashed them all.

*(Note—As this is written, Jack Warren and Barney Johns have left the hospital and are at Officers Candidate School at Fort Sill, Oklahoma. Kennard has begun to walk without a limp, thereby confounding all the doctors who attended him but not First Lieutenant Elizabeth Kennard of the WACS, formerly Third Officer Elizabeth Ware of the WAACS. Also, it is now necessary to address Jim as Captain Kennard.)*

This is Lieutenant Kennard s story of the little known, almost fabulous men of the forward observer detail, who penetrate to the farthes reaches of the battle fronts, with Death at thei shoulders. They are the Army's expendables Acting as the eyes and ears of the artillery, the work in groups of four, their job to find and giv the range of enemy targets.

FORWARD OBSERVER is the first authentic insid story of field artillery reconnaissance — a dra matic narrative of one daring group of mei under fire in the Tunisian campaign. Often thei heroic story reads like fiction. There was th tragic day when Lieutenant Kennard sentence his closest friend to death — to stop a Romme tank drive. There was the time Kennard an another scout were far behind the enemy line: The Nazis counter-attacked — leaving ther deep in hostile territory. But they had one ga interlude in Algiers — when Kennard an "Rick" both fell desperately in love with a prett WAC.

Written in swift, crackling prose, interlarde with irrepressible American humor, FORWAR OBSERVER is an unforgettable picture of Amer can fighting men in action.

This is a chart such as is used in the battalion Fire Direction Center. It shows the complete advance plan of artillery fires for a regimental attack. This chart is traced from the divisional or regimental map of attack. The Forward Observer must familiarize himself thoroughly with all details of this plan. New targets reported by him also will be plotted on the chart. Lines RZ-RZ and LZ-LZ mark the limits on the right and left sides of the regimental zone of action. The center line separates the zones of the two committed battalions. Each circle represents a target within which is the artillery concentration number assigned to it. BP is the Base Point and Ck Pt's the Check Points. The numerals which indicated units have been blocked out.

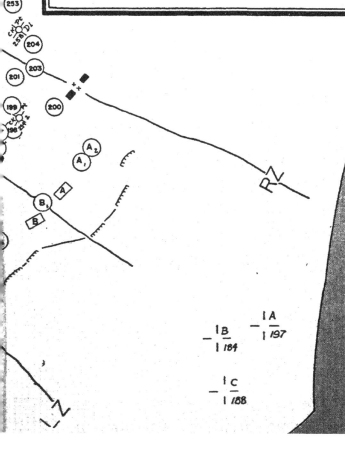

Lightning Source UK Ltd.
Milton Keynes UK
UKHW011822170722
405982UK00001B/17

9 781406 706369